P9-CMA-280

FINAL
Scenes

Bedside Tales at End of Life

JANET STARK

FINAL SCENES
Bedside Tales at End of Life

ISBN-13: 978-1-77069-125-4

Printed in Canada.

Word Alive Press
131 Cordite Road, Winnipeg, MB R3W 1S1
www.wordalivepress.ca

WORD ALIVE PRESS
Just Write!

Library and Archives Canada Cataloguing in Publication

Stark, Janet, 1955-
      Final scenes : bedside tales at end of life / Janet Stark.

ISBN 978-1-77069-125-4

      1. Hospice care. 2. Death. 3. Terminal care--Religious aspects--Christianity. I. Title.

R726.8.S694 2010   362.17'56   C2010-907219-7

This book is dedicated to
all our loved ones who
have gone on before us.

Many thanks to all the
generous people who have
shared their stories with me.

TABLE OF CONTENTS

Spiritual Needs at End-of-Life

"When Cure is not possible, Care is…"

TIPS & TOOLS FOR TEACHING & RULING ELDERS,
AND SPIRITUAL CARE TEAMS

A "Good" Death
When one:
- is at peace.
- is ready to "go home."
- is finished preparations.
- has no regrets.
- has a "healed" spirit.

Spiritual Distressors

- Losses
- Fear
- Guilt
- Pain
- Loneliness

ABOUT SPIRITUAL NEEDS

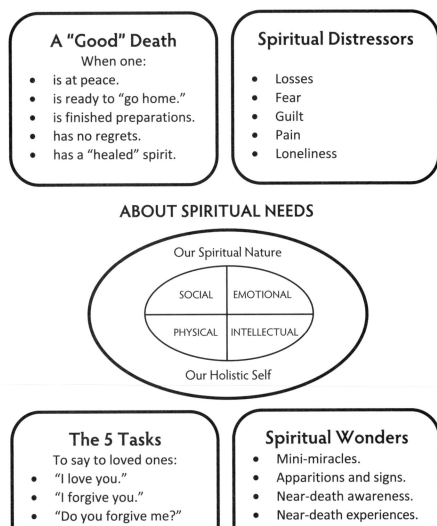

Our Spiritual Nature

| SOCIAL | EMOTIONAL |
| PHYSICAL | INTELLECTUAL |

Our Holistic Self

The 5 Tasks
To say to loved ones:
- "I love you."
- "I forgive you."
- "Do you forgive me?"
- "Thank you."
- "Goodbye."

Spiritual Wonders
- Mini-miracles.
- Apparitions and signs.
- Near-death awareness.
- Near-death experiences.
- Giving permission to "let go."

What Helps?

Spiritual Reminiscence
- Encourage storytelling.
- Let them know they will be remembered.
- Remind them of their value.
- Affirm legacy.

Do NOT Say...
You have to:
- "Hold up."
- "Be strong."
- "It's all in God's will."
- "There must be a blessing in all this."

Gifts of Self

Show Up!   Sincere Words
Agape Love   Gentle Touch
Mercy and Grace   Simple Prayer
Develop Trust   Serving Feet
Eye Contact   "Be" Rather Than "Do"

Helpful Practices
Listen!

Listen, Respect
Listen, Respond
Listen, Share
Listen, Encourage
Listen, Refer

Life After Death

Explore their beliefs.
How do they frame it?
- Heaven?
- Paradise?
- Eternal life?
- Everlasting life?

Do they welcome going to this place?
Are they afraid?

Helpful Tools
Prayer, Readings,
Music, Nature,
Ritual

One can die healed.
We do not have to walk alone.
Goodbye: "God-be-wi'ye"

INTRODUCTION

My first exposure to end-of-life care was more than thirty years ago, when my grandmother died. I had not yet been introduced to the concepts of palliative care or hospice care; in fact, I don't think these terms were even used back then. Grandma had reached the last days of a long and full life, and had been transferred from nursing home to hospital. My husband and I lived out of town, and it was just by chance we happened to be back home at this time.

We visited her just a few days before she died. I remember spending a short time with her, coming close beside her in the hospital bed, telling her I loved her and kissing her soft face. I don't think I was fully aware that she was dying or that I wouldn't see her again.

Soon, Grandma died. I was sad, but also pleased when I heard Grandma had asked to be buried in the dress my husband and I had bought for her a few months before. It was navy blue with little red hearts.

This experience of a "good death" must have had an influence on me. Years later, I became a coordinator of palliative care education for health professionals, and more recently, a spiritual care coordinator of a community hospital. I did not know where life's twists and turns would take me. I did not know the plans God had for me—how events, opportunities and training would fit together and lead me to a very fulfilling career helping those at end-of-life.

You may find these stories sad, but there are many funny moments within them. I believe that laughter and tears are very closely connected! It is my wish that you will not come away from the book sad, but with much to think about. It is my hope that by reading these stories, you will reflect on your own life, and of those you love, and find peace in knowing that God provides great comfort by equipping ordinary people to be His hands in the world. The tool He provides us with is the most healing of all. It is the gift of LOVE.

Grandma, I hope you are looking down and know that I still love you.

*"Count your many blessings, name them
one by one, count your many blessings,
see what God has done."*
—Old Hymn

A Baked Potata

I was paged to the ICU one afternoon and went quickly, not knowing what I would find. An older woman had been admitted and was under observation. Her son was just leaving, and I noticed that he leaned over and gave his mother a kiss on the lips. "I'll see you later," he said, and left. After introducing myself, Lenora patted the edge of the bed. I was grateful to sit down, and leaned forward to chat.

Lenora had come in "with a spell," as she called it. She seemed comfortable enough—the IV was running and the monitors were humming. She didn't seem at all anxious, and she didn't talk very much about her medical condition.

Lenora said to me, "I pray all the time, and if the good Lord wants to take me now, I'm ready to go." She smiled when she told me her husband had gone some years before. I asked about her children. She beamed with pride. "I have two sons and a daughter, and grandchildren too."

"Are they close by?" I asked.

Her face lit up. "Yes," she said. "One son lives on one side of me, my other son lives on the other side, and my daughter lives just down the road. I see my grandchildren lots of times." I remarked at how very lucky she was, to have her family settled so close. We talked about how this was almost unheard of today, as many families are scattered all over the world.

"Yes," she said. "I am so fortunate. I guess the young ones never wanted to leave their momma and papa."

She held my hand tight and we said prayers giving thanks for her life and asking for healing in whatever way God had planned for her. As I was about to leave, I asked if there was anything she wanted. "Well," she said, "what I really want is a baked potata."

When I went home that night, I put a potato in my briefcase.

"We are the clay, and You our potter;
And all of us are the work of Your hand."
—Isaiah 64:8

A Cracked Lamp

Patti told me this story: "At the time, I was in my thirties, the youngest of five kids.

Dad had lived with cancer for four years, and now was at the hospital near the end of his life. We were told he didn't have long left, and a week and a half later, he was gone, at age sixty-nine.

After he died, the family gathered back at the house. We are a big family with spouses and children, and I remember talking about my children, who were three and four at the time. Previously, one of my kids had accidentally cracked a ceramic lamp that belonged to Dad and Mom. It was one of a pair of hand-made ceramic lamps my sister-in-law had made as a gift for them. Dad had been annoyed that the lamp was broken, as it was special to him.

As we sat together talking in the living room, a strange thing happened. The light on the broken lamp came on and stayed lit for about ten seconds! After it went off, my brother said that something must be wrong with the lamp. I told him, "No, it was a sign that Dad was here with us in the room, and he was telling us he is all right."

There were mixed feelings about whether this were possible, but afterward, Mom said she thought I had been right. We checked the lamp switch. It had remained in the off position the whole time! After this event took place, that lamp continued to work just fine!

One foot is in the grave and the other
most definitely is in my running shoes.

A Death Sentence—Revoked

A feisty little lady told me this story. She is both a hospice volunteer and a spiritual care volunteer, has a wonderful sense of humour and is a prayer warrior. The devil will surely not catch her unaware!

Maureen had never been sick in her life. The only time she had been in hospital was for her babies—one regular delivery, four cesareans and a hysterectomy. She and her husband had had the same doctor for many years, but felt the need to make a change. They found a new doctor, and looking back, felt God had a hand in it.

One night at 4:00 a.m., she jumped out of bed, as she was very nauseous and felt like her body was on fire. She wondered if she had taken a stroke. The doctor prescribed antibiotics, but by Sunday, she was worse. She came into hospital by ambulance, and the priest was summoned to give her the sacrament of the living. All the tests were done by Wednesday, when the doctor told her she had a mass on her liver the size of an orange. She also had a mass on her gallbladder.

At first, Maureen did not say anything. After receiving the news, she chuckled, "My husband's been drinking since he was one-year old, and here's Mother Teresa lying here with a mass on her liver. Life is funny."

He responded, "Yes, life is funny."

Maureen never shed a tear. She told her family that if she could be fixed, they would fix her, but if not, then she would get ready for her next home. She was very weak, but not a bit nervous even though she was expecting to die.

Her family had enough tears to share. Although too sick to pray, a hymn refrain kept running through her head, "Be with me Lord for I am in trouble; Be with me Lord I pray."

She was transferred to a larger hospital, where a senior medical resident checked her all over very carefully. "What's your gut feeling?" asked Maureen.

"I don't have gut feelings," he replied. "I just have statistics."

"Well, what do your statistics tell you?" she asked.

"I think you have cancer," he replied.

She thought, "That's your opinion. I'll wait for a second one."

Maureen asked for a mild sedative that night. In the night, she woke up and looked at the window. There appeared a cross with clouds billowing around it. Three times, she turned and looked at the window, and the cross was there each time. She thought the Lord was telling her to prepare to come to heaven soon. She went back to sleep.

The liver specialist did a biopsy on a Thursday, and then Maureen wanted to go home. It was a holiday weekend, and no one wanted to take responsibility for releasing her. They told her they were afraid if she went home her liver would rupture. She smiled and said, "I'm not one bit afraid of my liver rupturing. I have this very good friend, and He's taking very good care of me." Maureen went home anyway.

The next week, she got the news that she had a very rare form of gall bladder cancer; in fact, less than one hundred people in the world had this type of cancer. She thought at that moment, "I must be special." She remembered the sign of the cross in the window, and believed God was preparing her to *bear her cross*.

That weekend, she changed her will and her power of attorney, and planned her funeral—right down to the music and the eulogy. This is where the story takes a twist.

A few days later, Maureen got a call telling her that THEY HAD MADE A MISTAKE, and read the tests wrong! The liver specialist was full of apologies! She had a follow-up CAT scan, and the results showed the mass on her liver at *half the size it was before*. A few months later, another scan showed the liver back to normal!

7

The following year, Maureen had an ultrasound, a barium enema and a colonoscopy, and all tests showed her organs to be completely healthy. She said to her family and her friends, "I AM A WALKING MIRACLE!"

I know this story is true, as I have seen the report! Maureen's sign of the cross in the window had actually been a sign for healing. Praise be to God!

"Blessed are those who mourn,
for they shall be comforted."
—Matthew 5:4

A Fine Young Man

Even those with great faith stumble at hardships in life, and we need to ask God to help us live moment by moment, even as we cannot make sense of it all. We shall reflect on the life of a young man who lost his life recently. These were some of the words spoken of him at his funeral.

We will remember this man with warmth and great fondness. As we cry, we will laugh. Through our grief, we will lift one another up in love and support, and through all this we will ask God to sustain us and comfort us, and surround us with His grace. I will attempt to describe some of the gifts that he possessed.

He was a unique character. God only made one of him! He was so intelligent. His Mom said he was an "Old Soul". He had a sense of wisdom and insight far beyond his years. He loved to read. He could read full sentences at three years-old. He read constantly and often all night, until he lost his eyesight.

He was musical. He loved an eclectic mix of music from classical, to heavy metal, to rock. He could play any instrument he laid his hands on. He wrote beautiful music and had his own band.

He was a skilled sportsman playing baseball and hockey. His Dad, who was the team coach, told us he learned to throw a curve-ball by going to the library and researching it when he was about ten years old.

He was a non-conformist. When his Mom tried to dress all her little boys in red-corduroy OshKosh overalls, he refused and took them off! As a teen, he wouldn't give in to peer pressure and had complete confidence in choosing his own path.

He had a sense of humour—he wore a dress to his high-school prom and his date wore a suit! This was not because he was *girlish*, but rather because he was different!

This man was so very ethical—He studied philosophy at University and told his parents he wanted to live an "ethical life." He was non-judgmental of all others. Even when he was a child, he formed the group "bully-busters" to protect little kids in kindergarten. He wanted to make the world a better place.

He was close to his family—a devoted older brother and son. His brothers spoke of good times when they were together. He had many long, deep conversations with his

Dad; they listened to CBC theatre together on Sunday nights. He was very respectful of his Mom, and all women. He loved animals. He was very loyal to his friends.

This young man was usually optimistic and would handle his troubles well. Unfortunately, due to a genetic flaw, he lost his eyesight about three years ago. When he lost his ability to read, and to use his computer musical programs, he lost a great strength. He struggled with the label "disability." His last few years included frustration, sadness and loneliness.

He was spiritual. Not in the manner of organized religion, but never-the-less, deeply spiritual. He believed in God and in life after death. The world may have failed him. I believe he has another world now. So what I suggest to the family and to all of you, is that you picture this fine man in heaven, amusing the angels with his music and his creative conversation, and staying up all night reading piles of books with his new, bright and clear eyes.

A friend is one who comes in when
the whole world has gone out.

A Fresh Face

Around the table sat fourteen new hospice volunteers in training. I was giving a presentation on *Spirituality at End of Life,* and I was looking around the room at each face. Facial expression is something I look for when I am speaking. I need that visual feedback in order to become animated in what I am saying. I guess I seek rapport with my audience. Perhaps that is why I would not be such an effective presenter if I were giving my talk on radio or in front of a camera.

As I looked from face to face, I noticed mostly older women, all with kind faces and soft smiles. There were three gentlemen in the class—a real bonus, because hospice care greatly benefits from having male caregivers. There are too few men who choose to volunteer in this sensitive area of health care.

The face that spoke to me most that evening was the enthusiastic and pretty face of a young woman. She was much younger than all the others. When the class was over, I asked to speak with her for a moment, and to tell me a bit about herself. She told me she was in training to be a nurse. Immediately, I told her I felt she was going to make a very good nurse! She turned her head a bit in question. I told her that not many young people are interested in gerontology, or end-of-life care. I said that this field is usually more attractive to a more *mature* person with life experience. She agreed with me, and told me that most of her classmates were interested in the more exciting fields of medicine: emergency, surgery, research, maternity and so on. She told me she had always been interested in older people, and wanted to learn about nursing them in their last days. I told her again that we were very lucky to be getting her as a new nurse; her enthusiasm and youthfulness would be a bright light to many.

She left smiling. I left hoping that when I need nursing care, I will be lucky enough to get a nurse like her.

*Hospice care is all about
living while dying.*

A Good Listener

A "seasoned" volunteer told me this story. "Seasoned" means he had been with the program for many years, and had become a "senior" some time ago. Volunteer programs rely heavily on the services of retirees; in fact, I often wonder what percentage of our country's volunteers is made up of senior citizens.

Anyway, back to my story. Herb told me this story over lunch in the hospital cafeteria, and I enjoyed watching his eyes crinkle in laughter. He and a lady volunteer used to visit patients together. The lady volunteer was very bubbly and very chatty. The two of them would poke their heads in a room and announce that they were making rounds visiting for pastoral care. (Those were the days when "spiritual care" was called *pastoral care*.)

One particular long-term patient was less than receptive to their cheerful "hellos." He mumbled and grumbled each time they visited, and finally he told the lady visitor that she just talked too much! Herb was somewhat amused. After his partner toned down her approach somewhat, the cranky patient was won over and eventually even looked forward to their weekly visits.

One day, Herb's partner was not with him, and he was visiting alone. His natural approach was much quieter. He entered a room and noticed the curtain had been pulled across, separating the roommates, so he pulled up a chair at the end of one of the beds. He spoke to the patient gently and told him he was just going to visit a while with him; he would sit quietly at his bedside and give him company. He assured the patient that he needn't respond to him if he didn't feel like it.

After what seemed like a quarter of an hour of silence, the roommate piped up from beyond the curtain, "He won't be answering you; he's been dead for an hour!"

Nothing conquers death like the
love of a mother for her child.

A Premonition

Lillian kept her newborn baby girl in a cot right next to her, beside the bed. It was a time when there was much worry about SIDS—Sudden Infant Death Syndrome—and Lillian worried about the baby.

Suddenly she heard a voice: "I gave her to you; I can take her back in a heartbeat." Lillian knew that God was speaking to her. She felt He was telling her that despite all her worrying, He was in charge. Then she felt an overwhelming sense of peace knowing that *God was in charge.*

When Lillian's next baby was to be born, the doctor gave her a date to come in, and suggested a C-section. Lillian had an immediate sense of the presence of death. She began to prepare her home as if she wasn't going to be returning.

When the baby was to be born, Lillian's doctor was just going home after a busy day. Lillian panicked, and her terrible premonition of dying was increased as now she was to have a different doctor looking after her. When she told her husband of her dread, he ran after the doctor who told him not to worry—the other doctor was just as good. Then her doctor went home.

Lillian prayed that she would see the baby before she died. Then she bargained, asking for fifteen more years of life to raise her child. Again she had that peaceful blanket come over her—of love, acceptance and overwhelming peace.

Another doctor tended her. The baby was born, and Lillian and the baby were just fine. Her own doctor came in the next day and greeted her with tears in his eyes. They never discussed it, but Lillian was sure he understood what she had meant when she told him of her premonition.

It is now many years later, and Lillian has long passed fifteen extra years.

*"…seek, and ye shall find; knock
and it shall be opened to you."*
—Matthew 7:7

A Sign

Ben and Bonnie were a very close couple and had a deep Christian faith. When Ben was admitted to hospital with abdominal pains, they felt it was just a temporary problem needing some quick attention. After exploratory surgery, the Doctor gave them the bad news that Ben was full of cancer, and that little could be done.

Ben and Bonnie were stunned. They were thrown into a place of overwhelming emotion. Immediately, they called on their greatest spiritual strength—their faith. Through a few days of constant conversation with God and with each other, they came to a place of acceptance.

Still, Bonnie prayed for healing. When their minister came to visit, Bonnie asked her if it was selfish to pray for healing for Ben, if healing was not part of God's plan. "Of course not!" was her response. "He desires that you pray for healing."

When I visited later that morning, I explained that healing happens in different ways. A person's body can fail and die, but the healed spirit does not die, but lives on. I saw the Bible on the bedside table and I pointed out a verse in Hebrews 11:13: "These all died in faith, not having received the promises..."

I asked Ben how he felt and he said he was focusing on his wife and how she was doing. Then he said she was focusing on God, and that God's strength comes through Bonnie and then to him.

Then Bonnie told me an amazing story. She is one who has always asked God for a sign, such as the number of steps to take or a four-leaf clover. Often, she has experienced a sign that the Spirit was with her. Bonnie was praying for a sign for Ben. She held her Bible and asked for a Bible verse that would speak to her. She hoped to find some words of scripture that would give her comfort. She opened the Bible at random and pointed to a verse. It was Mark 8:12. Incredibly, it said: "But Jesus sighed deeply in His spirit and said, 'Why does this generation seek a sign? Assuredly, I say to you, no sign shall be given to this generation'."

Bonnie was greatly encouraged by this verse, and pondered on its meaning. She feels that Jesus was telling her not to bother looking for a sign, because *He has been right with them both all along!* She is now assured that a sign isn't necessary. Jesus will walk with them both, no matter what the outcome for Ben is. She says the voice in the Bible verse is like a parent gently chastising his child, saying, "Don't keep asking for things; I'm in charge here, and I will take care of you; in fact, I already am."

I told them it was a wonderful way to frame it in their mind. I prayed with them, giving thanks for their faith, and left the room full of hope in a sad situation.

"Dying is not a failure;
failure is not living."
—Bernie Siegel

A Spicy Story

I love stories—telling them and hearing them. I hope when I am old and sick there is a kind soul who will sit by my bedside and read to me. It can be a letter, the daily news, the Bible, or even nursery rhymes. There is something very soothing about hearing the spoken word. When the reader has a soft, comforting voice, that is better still.

One of the spiritual care volunteers loves to read to patients. She is an older lady, and says she "has been around thirty-nine more than twice!" Regularly, she comes into the hospital, chooses a book from the library and sets off to read to someone. One day, she began to read a novel to a patient. The story started in right away with what she called "spicy material." It soon got hotter and hotter! The volunteer stopped reading and looked up at the patient. They both were a little pink in the cheeks! Without too many words, it seemed evident this particular story was making them both a bit uncomfortable. They decided to nix the erotic fiction and start over on something a little tamer!

For some of us,
the grave holds no fear.

Aunt Toots Sees Uncle Harold

It is a common phenomenon for one who is near death to report seeing the spirits of loved ones around their bed. While I can't fully explain it, I certainly accept it. This is one of the spiritual mysteries surrounding life and death. What the ill person sees, I accept as true. I do not explain it away by crediting the medication or the delirium or dehydration for causing these experiences, but instead accept it as real signs and wonders. This gift, I believe, has been sent to provide comfort and to help one journey through death and over to the over side. Many times, a patient near death will reach out and call the name of one who has already died. Is God giving them a glimpse of who is waiting for them in heaven? While I do not believe we are meant to seek out contact with the dead, I accept the presence of a departed soul as a gift.

When she was dying, my Great-Aunt Toots spoke of seeing Uncle Harold in the room, in a corner by the ceiling. Harold had been dead many years. I believe he was calling

23

her to come and join him—to not fear death and to let her spirit pass over the chasm between life and death. What do you think?

Beyond the grave is a mystery.

"Aura" of Death

Lorna is a health-care aide in a country nursing home. During her experience caring for palliative residents, it has become apparent she has been given a special gift. Lorna says she is not sure if she is *blessed or cursed* with this gift, as it has caused her quite a concern. Simply put, Lorna can tell when someone is about to die.

This is not in the usual way—from the medical signs and symptoms—it is something far more unexplainable. Lorna can *sense death*. I call it an *aura* of death. An *aura* is an intuitive sense or feeling that something is about to happen.

Lorna told me that one time she was at a party and was introduced to a man she had never met before. She immediately became alarmed, as she had that familiar smell come over her. She confided to her husband that she felt this man was going to die. She had no reasons to believe this, other than her past track record. Sure enough, within twenty-four hours, she got word that the man had died. Lorna has predicted many times that someone is soon going to die. This awareness, or aura, has been validated by her nursing team, and Lorna is now asked to use her special sense to help prepare families for what is happening.

He's gone back to the earth and
is now pushing up daisies.

Bought the Farm

Does anyone know where that saying came from? "He skidded so hard on that gravel that he almost *bought the farm*." I wonder, what does this term have to do with death? There are many euphemisms that we use to mean *dead,* and I wonder if it says something about our death-denying society. Are we not comfortable saying the words, "He died"? We say things like *expired, passed, resting* and so on, when we're being serious; and we say things like *pushing up daisies, six-feet under, kicked the bucket, cashed in, gave up the ghost,* and so on, when we're being not-so-serious.

The term—*bought the farm*—really intrigues me. So I *googled* it and found a number of different stories. There were some about buying a plot of land, not really a farm. One story explained that when someone died in military action, he had now bought his farm (burial plot). Another story said that when a farmer died, if he had a life insurance policy, then his death meant that he had *bought the farm*.

I wonder what *"sell the farm"* means.

"Communicate. If necessary, use words."
— St. Francis of Assisi

Bringing in the Cows

I first learned about dementia when I was twelve, and visited my Grandma in hospital. She had suffered a stroke and could no longer speak. But Grandma did not have dementia; her mind was very sharp, even though she could not verbally communicate. It was her elderly roommate who was confused. In those days, elderly confusion was called *senility*; the term *Alzheimer's disease* had not yet come to light (and by the way, the term is *Alz-heimer*, not *Old-timers*, or *All-timers*. I'm not sure why so many people have trouble with that).

Anyway, Grandma's roommate would get confused and would call out things such as, "It's starting to rain—get the clothes off the line," or "It's time to feed the chickens." I was reminded of this memory long stored away when I heard the following story.

An elderly woman was nearing end-of-life in a local nursing home. She was more often confused than not, due to advanced dementia and possibly delirium. One night, it was storming outside, raining very hard. The night nurse was trying to calm her, as she seemed very agitated and worried about things.

The lady told the nurse, "I have to go out and bring in the cows. They can't stay out in this storm." The night nurse very kindly tried to reason with her that all would be well, but her patient's agitation escalated.

Finally the nurse got an idea. She told the lady, "Don't worry, you stay here and I'll go out and bring in the cows." Then she put on her trench coat and went outside long enough to get it wet. She came back into the patient's room and, taking off her wet coat, said, "Yes, I got all the cows into the barn; I even managed to get the bull in, too."

Suddenly, very intensely aware, the little lady in the bed said, "Since when did Dad get a bull?!!"

If you are a leaf on the tree of life,
when autumn comes you will fall
in glorious colour.

Bucket List

One of my favourite movies is *The Bucket List,* starring Jack Nicholson and Morgan Freeman. They have great chemistry when working together. These two men are both sharing a room in hospital, and both are dying from cancer. They discover together that before they die, there are certain things they would like to do. They haven't yet fulfilled all their dreams and wishes, and have places to see before they *kick the bucket.* Of course, the make-believe nature of their illness allows them to be perfectly well enough to go on a major adventure together!

They travel the world, climbing pyramids and mountains, while spending an exorbitant amount of money. The movie is both very funny and very sad, and teaches a very important lesson about dying with no regrets.

If you were to write your *bucket list*, what would be on it? Included on my list are these things: I want to sleep overnight in the sleeper car of a moving train. I also want to sleep in the sleeping cab of an eighteen-wheeler truck. (I have a fixation on sleeping!) I want to go to Scotland, and to a small island near Madagascar named Mauritius.

A friend of ours who was diagnosed with a debilitating illness went out and bought a convertible sports car. He and his wife have had so much fun in it. What would be on your bucket list? What is keeping you from getting started?

*If you take good care of yourself, then I
know you will take good care of me.*

Care for the Caregivers

A well-beloved nurse died recently on the same floor where she had worked for many years. Staff members were recently upset during a murder trial because one of their colleagues had been killed. The staff was in crisis when they heard alarming news that one of their own had lost a child to suicide. Add to this the normal incident of grieving for one's patient who has died.

In providing a good spiritual care program for patients in hospital, we often overlook the needs of staff. Nurses need an opportunity to grieve and to express feelings and concerns. I recently learned that a nearby long-term care home had more than eighty residents die last year. With all of this going on, nurses are expected to get up out of bed the next day, come to work with cheerful attitudes and be productive.

Spiritual Care services have to provide care for staff as well as patients. If the workers are well-cared for, then it stands to reason that they in turn can provide better care.

We have been called to do staff de-briefings, last-minute prayer services, memorial services and even funerals.

A de-brief is a time for reflection, meditation, prayer, and expression. The team gathers strength in knowing that they are united in their concerns or losses. It helps validate the stress level among the staff.

Another thing, of which we should all be aware, is that nurses bring their own family concerns with them. They may be experiencing difficulties, health problems in their families and personal grief and loss. Even for a professional, it is hard to separate this personal weight when arriving at work to care for others. Let us remember to view the caregiver as a *whole person*, in the same way we do the patient.

"Even the lilies of the field are
arrayed in more splendor
than Solomon's finest."
—Matthew 6:29

Chaplain in Shorts

How does one recognize a chaplain? One might expect a black jacket, white clerical collar and perhaps a cross. Whether we are referring to priest, pastor or minister, we are used to having these symbols to identify the profession.

One day, I arrived at my office to find one of my volunteer chaplains checking over the patient lists. He was wearing a short-sleeved shirt and a pair of shorts. I didn't think anything of it. He told me that his wife had been admitted to hospital with a case of vertigo, and after getting her comfortably settled, he decided to see if there were any patients who would benefit from a visit.

After he went on his way, I decided to pay a visit to the chaplain's wife. After I inquired about her condition, she asked the whereabouts of her husband. "He's not out doing hospital visits, is he? I told him he couldn't go round the hospital in his shorts!" she said. I said that I thought he was doing just that! The wife said that he was in hospital to look after her, and not in a professional capacity today. I told her that I'm sure the Lord (as well as the patients) loves knobby knees!

I may be old,
but I'm not dead!

Checking Out the Ladies

Not only do men and women grieve differently, but each individual grieves differently. One who has lost a spouse of many years may have a difficult journey working through their grief until they reach a stage of relative wellness.

I say *relative* intentionally, as this degree of wellness is indeed very subjective. When my father-in-law lost his wife, he never quite returned as a whole, happy spirit. A piece of him was gone forever. In contrast, I know of a fellow who lost a wife of many years, and within months was finding regular company with a new friend.

Long gone is our old paradigm that one must grieve for a year in order for the grief to appear seemly and proper by society. Each person follows his own path, and we try not to give too many directions! A man who seeks female companionship after losing a wife, does not mean that he has loved his wife any less. Some men need the nurturing touch of a woman; in fact, they might readily admit they need a woman to take care of them!

I remember our bereavement coordinator telling the story of a widower who came to her grief support group. He was dressed spiffily in a plaid sports jacket (picture Don Cherry)! In being welcomed into the group, he told the facilitator that he knew there would be widows in the group and "he was there to check out the ladies!"

He had a totally different concept of grief support! As this was not a dating service, the facilitator told me she hid the registration list that had the ladies' phone numbers on it!

Laughter is free medicine.

Clowning Gone Bad

I am privileged to do chaplaincy work in a hospital that provides palliative and long-term care. I have an eclectic skill set, which includes being a lay minister and a care clown. They work together, don't they? I enjoy letting my hair down, dressing up, and goofing off in order to bring smiles to the patients. Laughter can bring a needed change of outlook to those who are suffering. It is rewarding to interact, first in a silly way, and then softening down into a caring and loving manner. I usually go visiting room to room, spending just a few moments with silly gags and leaving with words of encouragement.

That was my plan last Halloween. Heading down the hall on the third floor, things were going very nicely until I was foiled by a little old lady who had dementia. One look at me and she wagged her finger and said, "I'm not giving you any candy. All you do is put pins in apples for little kids!"

Well, that took the air out of my balloon pretty quick! I murmured something and backed out of her room with a dumb look on my face. The nursing staff thought it quite hilarious that I had just been told off!

As I waited for the elevator, along came the little lady shuffling along in her wheelchair. "I'm so sorry, I'm so sorry I was so miserable," she said. That put a big clown smile back on my face!

*"Goodbye" comes from the
Gaelic: "God–be-wi'-ye"*

Coming Home

Dad was dying. He was a retired farmer from Southern Ontario, and he was dying of lung disease. One spring day, we got *the call*. It was my Mom, asking us to come to Hamilton to the hospital. Dad had gone on oxygen a few days before, at home, and now his condition was worsening. At one point his heart had stopped, and with a flurry of activity, he was revived.

At the time, the doctor didn't know he had a handwritten advanced directive with a *do not resuscitate* order. In retrospect, my Mom said it was just as well, as giving him a few more days of life allowed us to say our goodbyes. All five children made it home, and at one time all of us were in the hospital room with Dad. We're spread out now, and it's not often we are all together. Dad knew he was dying. I had written him a poem, thanking him for all of the things he taught me over the years.

To Dad

Dad, over the years you taught me many things:
To play euchre, checkers and crokinole
To dance, and enjoy fiddle music
To make homemade ice cream
To like black licorice and humbugs
How to braid bindertwine for a calf rope
To swing on a rope in the barn
How to write a speech about Wilf Carter
To sing to the cows: "Mares Eat Oats",
   "Little Brown Jug",
"Turkey in the Straw" and "Cheer Boys Cheer"
To enjoy a country picnic
How to feed a dog from the table
A strong work ethic; (I picked stones)
To take interest in my family history
To take pride in the love of the land
For all these things I am grateful—
I love you, Dad.
Janet

Dad was not an emotionally expressive man, but as I read him the poem that night, he squeezed my hand so hard. Without words, I knew he loved me, and he had given me the blessing. He said *"thank you"* and it was more than enough.

One afternoon, we all went down to get a snack and give Dad some quiet time. When we returned, his minister was there. The minister had my poem in his hand. They must have been chatting about us kids, because I heard my Dad say, *"I guess we didn't do too bad, because all my kids came home to see me"*. The minister was doing what we call in palliative care: *giving meaning and purpose by a life review*.

Over the next few days, there was lots of family going in and out of that room, and at one point we thought he had rallied and was improving. When the doctors discussed palliative care with my parents, it was then Dad said he wanted to go home. The weekend was coming, and it was going to be hard to arrange his discharge with home nursing care. It was month-end as well, and the doctors were on monthly rotation. He was getting a new doctor. We promised him we would get him home.

He held on—weak with very laboured breathing, and not able to eat much. Late Tuesday afternoon, the ambulance brought him home. As the attendants carried the stretcher into the old stone home, he had them stop and he took a long last look at his farm. He looked at the fields and the rolling hills, the barn and the home where he had brought my Mom as a new bride fifty-five years before. Again, he said *"thank you"*. They put him into the hospital bed, which had been prepared in the living room. Then it quieted down. My Mom was with him, and also my sister, a geriatric nurse. Perfect. His breathing changed, and with my Mom and my sister holding his hands, he died about an hour-and-a-half after he got home. It was *perfect*. He had come home, to his beloved farm, to die.

43

*"Better to have loved and lost
than never to have loved at all."*
—Alfred Lord Tennyson

Crayons for the Coffin

One of the health educators for the palliative care program told this story. A young man was dying of AIDS. As you can imagine, this was very hard on the family. There is still a stigma in many parts of the country about AIDS and homosexuality, and all of the issues that accompany those things. Mostly, the family was devastated to be losing a devoted son. A child is not supposed to die before a parent.

His wish was to die at home, and in the young man's last days, there were many people coming in and out. The family members were each in different stages of what we call *anticipatory grief*. The father, especially, was having great trouble expressing his feelings. He was filled with a sharp, raw grief and confused about expressing it. This man was a very creative fellow; he had always done beautiful wood-working with his hands.

The health educator was also a counselor, and he was visiting the young man one day. They talked easily about approaching death. It became apparent that the young man had a few very simple wishes around his funeral and burial. One was that he be buried in a simple wooden coffin. He wanted lots of coloured crayons available, so all his friends and nieces and nephews could colour and write messages on his coffin! What an idea! He wanted those who loved him to be able to leave him with a message of hope that creative design brings.

They explained this plan to the father, who nodded his head and said little. Then, as his son lay dying in the bedroom, he quietly went down to his woodworking shop and began hand-crafting a coffin—his son's coffin. This was the missing piece, an avenue for him to express his pent-up emotions in a creative way. His son soon died, and the funeral was just as the young man wished, with singing and celebration and lots and lots of brightly-coloured messages on the simple wooden coffin. By the time he was buried, the grieving process was well underway.

"Life is not a dress rehearsal."
—Rose Tremain

Dance with the One Who Brung Ya

There is an old saying that if a girl went out to a dance with a fella, she had better remember to *Dance with the one that brung ya.* In other words, don't be giving your attention to anyone except your date.

I think of Phyllis, a little lady in hospital awaiting a long-term care bed. Phyllis looked to be in fairly good health, but she had no short-term memory and she was a wanderer. She seemed content in her surroundings and was usually in quite good spirits. She loved to visit with anyone who would give her the time. She would pat the chair or the bed beside her and say, "Sit down for awhile."

The volunteers always brought Phyllis to chapel service. She would ask if her hair was all right and if she needed a sweater, and if it was a long ride. Even though we were just taking her to another part of the hospital, she brought her purse. I always thought it was so cute when she patted the chair beside her and told the volunteer, "You sit with me."

After the service was over, she looked for *her* volunteer, and said she was going back home with the one that brought her. I smiled when she met with her roommate on the elevator and asked, "Are you goin' to my place or am I coming over to yours?" She had forgotten they were already roommates.

It is certainly a huge loss to develop a major memory deficit in older age. But Phyllis showed me that you can make the best of it, living and enjoying each moment. I regretted that in my role as program director, I didn't have time just to sit and be with her. Perhaps when I retire, I can take this time as a volunteer. When she pats the chair and says, "Sit for awhile," I am going to do just that.

If we could all have
the faith of a dog!

Doggies with Red Scarves

My office sits near the entrance to the hospital, so a great deal of traffic goes by my door. Sometimes I look up from my desk and see who is going by, and sometimes I answer inquiries or give directions. I don't really mind. I always have a smile for the visitors, as I know each of them carries a story, and sometimes it is a difficult one.

Quite regularly, I look up from my desk as I hear someone pass by, and see four furry legs alongside the owner. I love to see these dogs come into the hospital. I firmly believe that animals are bona fide caregivers and often more successful than we are in health intervention. Scientific studies have found that when an ill person pats a gentle dog, blood pressure and breathing rates go down.

If I catch a glimpse of a red scarf on the doggie, I know it is a trained dog from *therapeutic paws*. Almost always, I scoot out from behind my desk to say hello to the *volunteer*. If patting a dog puts a smile on my face and helps me

48

have a better day, then imagine what it might do for someone sick or dying?

Sometimes the dogs visit the dementia day-care unit, at other times the long-term care residents, or the palliative patients. I have seen dogs of all colours and sizes, from great big collies to little tiny dachshunds. They all know the drill of the hospital routine and are on their best behaviour. When I am sick and dying, I hope that there will be a dog on the health team to take care of me.

"Sometimes the physician's job is just to amuse the patient while nature takes its course."
—Voltaire

Dying Healed

One of my favourite Bible verses is Hebrews 11:13. It is about not receiving our rewards in this life. Paraphrased, it says all these people were still living by faith when they died. They did not yet receive the things promised.

There is a marked difference between curing and healing. When one reaches the palliative stage of life, we can say that *curing* is no longer possible, but we can still *care.* I have always said that at this point, we can focus on dying *healed.* The chaplain I work with says, "There are worse things than dying," and I am inclined to agree with him! When we talk of a *good* death, we are usually describing a situation where the person has found peace and has let go of any baggage and unfinished business.

The best teacher of the *dying healed* concept, I believe, is Dr. Ira Byock. He is a well-known palliative care physician in Missoula, Montana. In his book *Dying Well*, he explains that a dying person needs to complete five tasks. Quite simply, he needs to tell his loved ones that he loves them, he forgives them and that he asks for forgiveness too, and then he says thank you and goodbye. An entire lesson on *dying healed* can be developed from these concepts.

A believer who is dying may not be afraid and may even embrace death. He may look forward to meeting his Lord and being united with his loved ones. He also looks forward to receiving his heavenly reward and his new body, whole and now free from all illness. What a tremendous hope, that when we die, we can be healed!

Our lives are just out on
loan from God's library.

Five Dollar Bill

Teaching health ethics can be a dreary task. When I present this topic to health professionals and volunteers, I tell them that I will do my best not to bore them! Then I try to live up to my promise.

The basic principles include: beneficence/non-malificence, dignity, autonomy, justice, and sanctity of life.

To illustrate the *sanctity of life* concept, I ask someone to hand over a $5 bill. Sometimes I have to coax, but there is always one who will bite. Then I ask the group, who would like to have this $5 bill? At least the person who gave it to me raises his hand!

Then I take it and crumple it up in my hand. "Who would like it now?" I ask, holding it up. Always, a few are interested. Next I put it on the floor and stomp on it. It is still crumpled up, and by now it looks really shabby. "Who would be interested in having this $5 bill now?" There is always a taker.

So finally, I take the bill and tear it right down the middle until it is only hanging together by a thread. "And now?" I ask. First of all, they are usually stunned that I would do that to perfectly good money— money that is not even mine! Always someone says, "I'll have it."

The point I then make with the class is that *where there is breath, there is life, and where there is life, there is value.* This $5 bill, though in very bad shape, is still worth a full $5. I then explain that an ill person, even when in a geri-chair, semi-conscious and needing to be fed and totally cared for, still has value.

I let that sink in for a while. Then I get the tape.

They can take my body,
but they can't kill my spirit.

Five Stickies

As we travel through life, we grieve many losses. We grieve losing our first tooth, or our favourite primary school teacher. We grieve losing our ability to skip and jump as we grieve losing our youth. Some of us grieve losing our hair, and maybe again we grieve losing all our teeth! At some point, we face the loss of our health. The normal life cycle consists of a series of losses.

To illustrate this point, I have the members of a class take five small yellow sticky-notes, and on each one, write something they have in their life that is very meaningful to them. It could be their new car, their flower garden, their ability to play golf, or their dog. Most often, it is more profound things such as their spouse, family, health or faith.

I ask them to put these five stickies on each finger of their left hand. With their right hand, I ask them to take a sticky from their neighbour. I tell them they don't care which one they take, as they aren't really interested in what it is. They set it down in front of them, and then they turn to their neighbour again, and take something else. Now each one has only three stickies left. Once more, they do the same thing, removing a sticky from their neighbour. When finally they each have only one thing left, I tell them they can stop.

Then I describe this scenario: You are eighty years-old, and have been coping fairly well at home on your own, until one day you have a stroke. Your children try to take care of you for a while, as best they can. One day they gather together and tell you how sorry they are, but that you will need to move into a care home.

You have arrived at the new nursing home, lonely and bewildered and suffering from limited movement from your stroke.

This is where the *stickies* come in. I ask the class what things they have lost. As they describe the kinds of things they lost, I add to the story.

Now you can't get out to church and you miss it so, and all your church friends, too. No longer can you drive, as your license has been taken away. You miss your old farmhouse where you spent many happy years, and your prize-winning flower garden. You miss your home-cooked meals because now you can't chew and swallow properly and are getting a minced diet. You are not over the loss of your husband, who died two years ago, and not only do you miss him, but you miss your cat, Spooky.

Then the Doctor comes in and tells you that the stroke has left permanent damage, and you will not walk again.

The next week more test results come in, and the Doctor comes back in with more bad news. You also have a chronic illness, the beginnings of Parkinson's disease.

That's quite enough losses. I now ask the class members how they feel. The answer is "pretty bad." I ask them to respect a person's losses when they are caring for them. It is not just about the physical condition you are caring for today, it is also about a series of losses that led up to this point. This helps sensitize staff and volunteers in understanding the complex needs of a person with declining health.

Then I ask the class members to share what last item they were left with—the last sticky on their finger. Then we discuss how to foster a sense of hope, having at least something of value left on which to build spiritual strength.

This story of loss is not rare; these are real cases of real folks we deal with every day. Let us learn more loving ways to provide care when the one we are caring for is so vulnerable.

"You light up my life;
you give me hope to carry on."
—Debby Boone

Flickering Light

I love this romantic story that was shared with me recently.

My father-in-law was a Scotsman, an architect and a veteran of World War II for Britain. He met and married my mother-in-law in India, where her father worked for the British government as an accountant.

Theirs was a love story of legend, and to the last second of his life he worshipped the ground she walked on. When she spoke, his eyes never left her face. I had noticed this for years and always thought it was so sweet.

I was lucky enough to be at the hospital when my father-in-law passed away. He had never been in hospital a day in his life, and at eighty-three found himself with a broken hip from which he would never recover. He had been in a coma, so they said, but I found that he responded with a hand squeeze to let me know he could hear all that was happening. I also saw tears in his eyes at times. He died with his beloved wife at his side, staring lovingly into her eyes until the very end.

The next day, all the family gathered at the family home as we comforted my mother-in-law, shared stories and made funeral arrangements. I was sitting in a chair facing the master bedroom, which was at the end of the hallway.

Suddenly, I saw a light flickering on and off continuously. I waited, thinking it would stop, but it didn't. I nudged my husband who looked and saw it as well. This went on for a few minutes while my mother-in-law was talking. When there was a pause, I asked her if she was having problems with the lamp in her bedroom and she said "no." I mentioned the light flickering on and off, but being a very practical and no- nonsense person, she passed it off, I believe, as over-imagination or wishful thinking on my part. Later I discovered that the flickering light was on the side of the bed where my father-in-law always slept.

I went and checked the bulb and the switch, but found no evidence of a problem. I told my children, sister and brother-in-law about it and I said that it was Granddad letting us know that he is okay and is still present.

It is my belief that our departed loved ones are with us daily and sometimes, if we really pay attention and are very lucky, we will see the signs and feel their presence. I believe that this is God's way of comforting the grief-stricken and reassuring us that there is indeed an afterlife.

*She was being so noisy I thought
she could raise the dead!*

"Gordon, Get Back Here!"

Gillian flew out to Victoria to visit her brother-in-law, who was dying. She was also there to support his wife, Diane, who was having a hard time accepting things. Diane had called the kids to come back to Victoria to see their father one last time. Gillian offered to sit at the bedside while Diane went to the airport to pick up their daughter.

The nurse looked in on Gordon, and then told Gillian that Diane better come back right away, so Gillian phoned her on her cell phone, and reached Diane who was now only about ten minutes from the airport. Gillian told her what the nurse had said, but Diane replied she had to get her daughter, but would come back as soon as they could.

Gordon took his last few breaths, and then died. Gillian was so distraught that she yelled at him, "Gordon! You can't die! *I told Diane you would be right here when she got back!*"

Suddenly, Gordon came back from the dead and opened his eyes! The nurse was astonished! She had never seen this happen before. In the meantime, Diane called the airline and she got her daughter right off the plane, and back to the hospital. The other children arrived, too, and Gordon lived for three more days!

Gillian had wondered if she had done the right thing—bringing him back. Would that mean more suffering? Then she decided that getting to have all his family around him one last time was a real gift.

Near the end, there were many family members in the room—one from each generation: his wife, daughter, grand-daughter, brother and nephew. By chance, a young lady came into the room carrying a bouquet of flowers. She gave one to each family member. There were fourteen people in the room and exactly fourteen flowers. Soon after, Gordon died—again.

The taste of death is sweet for
those who long to be with the Lord.

Hallelujah!

Nadia's parents had been missionaries to India. Nadia had gone to boarding school and then trained to be a nurse. She told this story of her mother's death.

When Mother was dying of cancer, we were all at the bedside—my brother, my father and myself. Mother was not afraid, because she had made her peace with God. Because she was not afraid, we were not afraid either. We were just sad to be losing her.

I remember the bed was partially reclined, and suddenly mother sat straight up. She looked to the corner of the room as if her eyes were fixated on something there. Her face seemed to glow with excitement—or expectation. As we watched intently, she cried out in a voice full of joy, "HALLELUJAH!!" Then she fell back in the bed and died."

God works in mysterious ways,
His wonders to perform…

Healed Tree

My Aunt Carrie told me her story of *The Healed Tree:*

My Mother planted the tree in the backyard because there was no air-conditioning, and we needed shade to cool the house from the afternoon sun. The tree grew quite big, and as Mother's health failed, I would take her out to sit on the back patio. She would always ask, "Where's my tree?" She loved looking at that tree.

There was a terrible storm one night, many years after Mother died. I saw a flash of lightning and I heard a big crack—it sounded like it was right outside my window. I got up to let my little dog Natalie out, and at the same time I pulled up the blind in the sunroom to have a look.

Mother's tree was sliced right down the trunk, with the bark all pulled away and just hanging by the bottom. You could see all the white splintered shards of wood broken from inside the trunk. There seemed to be a bright light all around the tree. I wondered, "Where is that spotlight shining from?"

The first thing I thought of, was how much it would cost me to have that tree cut down—maybe a thousand dollars! "Oh God," I prayed, "What am I going to do, I do not have a thousand dollars!" I went back to bed.

In the morning, I went out in the back yard to look at the damaged tree. It was completely intact! There was no damage at all! I looked to see if there was a seam in the wood, and it was completely smooth. It was incredible! God healed my tree! He healed my tree because He knew I didn't have a thousand dollars!

I told this story to a friend who knew it had been my Mother's tree. She asked me if I thought my Mother had anything to do with it. "Maybe your Mother is looking after you," she said.

*"They shall see His face, and His name
shall be on their foreheads."*
—Revelation 22:4

Hiding His Face

Karen was a new chaplain at a large city hospital. One day, she was called to the ICU, as they had a man in distress. She quickly climbed the stairs, saying her usual prayers for guidance. When she arrived, she was greeted by the nurses who told her that she was greatly needed to help gain the cooperation of their patient.

A big, burly man had collapsed at the gas station two days before. He had been unconscious for two days, and they were not sure if he would survive. Now he was awake, but was very agitated. Every time the nurses went near him, he put his hands over his face. They needed to tend to him, to take tests and do procedures, but every time they approached him, he put his hands over his face.

They were hoping Karen could help. "What do you want me to do?" she asked. She had no idea how to proceed with this gentleman. Her training did not prepare her for anything like this! So after she introduced herself to the patient, she sat for awhile in silence at the end of his bed. After a while, he peeked through his fingers, saw she was still there, and then covered his face. Again, this repeated itself. Karen stayed silent, all the while being very aware that the nursing staff was anxious to get going with his care.

Finally, Karen asked him, "What do you need? The nurses want to help you, but you won't let them near you. Tell me what you need."

Cautiously, he lowered his hands a bit and said, "You will laugh at me." After Karen promised not to laugh, he finally started. "I don't know where I am, or what day it is." He was confused and frightened. More information came—he was most worried about his dog that had been left alone in his townhouse. He was late with the rent. He had written a cheque for the landlord, but it was back at the gas station in his van.

Karen told him she would take care of things, and explained what she would do. She asked him if he would let the nurses take care of him now, and the patient nodded his head. Then she drove to the gas station, got the rent cheque, went to the landlord and told him what had happened. The landlord was most concerned and promised to take care of the dog, and sent a message back to the patient not to worry about anything until he got better.

Sometimes, providing *spiritual care* goes above and beyond what is in the standard job description. Sometimes it involves doing just about anything that will calm the fears and anxieties of a patient in distress.

Faith is good insurance; it has healing properties and the price is free.

Insurance—Reassurance

Matthew died of a brain tumour when he was twenty-nine years-old. In eleven months he had endured three surgeries, chemotherapy and radiation before he succumbed to his illness.

Two days after Matt's funeral, his older sister Barbara was having trouble sleeping, as her emotions were *totally fried*. As she dozed in and out of sleep, she had her hand extended in the air. She realized she was holding her brother's hand while he was leaning against a pool table. She could hear him say, "Tell Mom my life insurance is with Manulife."

In the morning, not sure if she had been dreaming, Barbara called her mother. She told her that Matthew had visited her in the night and informed her about a life insurance policy he owned.

In tears, her mother responded with her own story of events that also took place the previous night. She explained that a clock Matt had made for her when he was seven years-old started ticking. It had never worked.

They both believe Matthew's spirit had visited them to help put their minds at ease. The family had been unaware of any insurance. This life insurance policy was found, just as he had said. It was more than enough to pay for his funeral.

A few years later, Barbara was in hospital visiting another friend who was in kidney failure. She needed some time to collect her thoughts and went into the family waiting room. A woman she had never met before came up to her, brushed her knee and said, "Matthew wants you to know he is okay, and he would really like an *Oh Henry* bar."

Barbara was totally shocked at this comment, as this had been his favourite candy bar. She believed it was indeed another message from Matthew, as he had spoken to her once before.

Barb told me this story one evening over a glass of wine. I was still pondering on it the next morning. The piece that puzzles me is about the *Oh Henry* bar. (I am particularly fond of chocolate in any form.) If Matt was asking for a chocolate bar, does that mean there isn't going to be any chocolate in heaven? Since *Oh Henry* was Matt's favourite, I would rather believe that he used it as a means to connect with Barb and confirm that he was indeed speaking to her. I would also like to believe that Matt—in Heaven—was just on his way to get one.

"And now abide faith, hope, love, these
three; but the greatest of these is love."
—1 Corinthians 13:13

"I Love Ya, Kid."

My name is Patti, and I was *the kid*, the youngest of five children. The others say I was the most spoiled, but I don't think so!

After Dad died, I took it hard. There were other losses in the family; grandparents who had died, and cousins who had lost children, but for me, none mattered like the loss of my father. I was mad at God and mad at the world. Things just did not make sense to me. My Mom was worried about me. She had heard about a *spiritual reader* and encouraged me to go.

When we met, the spiritual reader only knew my first name. She took my hands in hers, and said a prayer to God. Then she released my hands. She said that she felt the spirit of an older man present and that he had a message for me.

"He says to you, 'You know I love ya, kid.'" I was blown away!

Dad was never able to come right out and say, "I love you," to me. He always said in an off-hand sort of way, like "You know I love ya, kid." Dad's spirit was indeed present, and it was such an encouragement to me!

Next, the spiritual reader told me to stand up, and then she told me that Dad wanted a *side hug*. Oh my gosh, I was just blown away again! Dad had always given me a side hug—he never felt comfortable giving me a straight-on hug, face to face! Again, I was greatly encouraged! Dad was all right, and he wanted me to be all right, too! There were tears running down my face. If Dad was at peace, then I could be, too! I was then able to forgive God, and move on with my life.

I want to die with my boots on.

Is It Okay to Smoke
While You're Dying?

An elder from our church preached a sermon many years ago, and I remember this question: He asked if God thought it was okay to smoke while you were praying. My first reaction was, "Well no—that's not very respectful."

Then he turned it around, and asked if God thought it was okay to pray while you were smoking. That changed my thinking completely! Of course, God would be pleased if you were smoking and then decided you would like to pray! Ponder on that for a minute.

I had been working for a few weeks with a family whose mother was in hospital. The daughter often checked in with me to provide me with an update of her mom's condition and to receive a few words of encouragement. The family needed to know that they were doing a very good job supporting the mom.

One morning, I was walking down the hall and the daughter caught up with me and asked if we could talk. "Sure" was my easy response.

"OK, well, I'm going outside for a smoke, and you can join me, it that's okay with you," she said. I told her I would just stop in to my office and pick up my coat. "Don't bother, she said, "It's a nice sunny day, and we won't be that long." So I chuckled to myself as I stood outside with her as she had her smoke. Smokers are pretty hard-core when it comes to putting up with all kinds of weather in order to satisfy their habit. But there I was, listening to her concerns, with my arms folded about me.

I was reminded that day of a case many years ago when I was a student on placement in hospital. I was an observer in a family conference, and the patient was dying with lung cancer. She was a smoker. Her daughter was with her for support. The health team was very focused on therapeutic goals for this woman, and reminded her of the perils of continuing to smoke in her condition.

Even though I didn't have any palliative care training, it occurred to me that they should let the woman alone. She was dying, and she enjoyed her cigarettes. I didn't think making her quit at this point would change the outcome at all, and I didn't think it was a very fine idea to take away the one thing that still gave her pleasure. I remember the upset expression on the daughter's face, and I was thinking that preparing her for her mom's death might be a better "therapeutic goal."

Smoking always comes up in volunteer training. To assist or not to assist when the patient wants to go outside to smoke, is the question we discuss. Most volunteers tell me they would assist a patient going for a smoke. They reserve any judgment in condemning a bad habit in one who is dying. The volunteers exhibit the attitude of *grace* toward the patient, and sometimes I think some health professionals could learn a thing or two from them.

*"Dying of a broken heart" can mean
dying from an emotional wound, or it
can mean dying from a worn-out
heart—or in some cases, both at once.*

Joined at the Hip

This is Lynn's story:

My dad passed away suddenly in 1999 from heart failure. My step-mother passed away seven hours later. She had been in a coma all night and never knew that her beloved husband had died after hearing the news by telephone that his adored wife was dying and would only live a few hours more. The hospital had called around midnight, and he had died within an hour of hearing the news.

Needless to say, I was completely bereft at the thought of both of them dying alone with no one there to hold their hand and console them.

The only comfort I found was that neither of them would have to deal with the death of the other and that they were, and are, together. I firmly believe that one could not have lived without the other for any length of time. They were, as the expression goes, *joined at the hip*.

I put on a brave face, but often found myself in tears of regret because I, whom my dad had always counted on to be there for him, was not there when he needed me most. The guilt and grief was overwhelming at times. I did my best to carry on, but there were times when it all flooded to the surface unexpectedly.

As they say, time heals all wounds, or at least it helps us to gain some relative peace and the ability to see things in a different light. I knew my dad and step-mother would be sad to know that I was suffering from these pangs of guilt. They would both want me to be happy now that they are together forever. This thought slowly replaced the guilt, and I realized that if my dad had lived, he would have eventually had to go into a long-term care home. It would have been a very unhappy existence.

Last year, on October 27, ten years to the day when my dad and step-mother died, I was folding laundry in my bedroom, thinking fondly of the two of them when suddenly the smoke alarm gave two very loud beeps.

This was very strange, as it had never happened before. Within seconds I realized that it was a sign from my dad, who had been captain of the fire department in the town where he lived his whole life! Dad had always emphasized strongly the importance of having smoke alarms and an escape plan, especially having seen many tragedies in the years he was a fireman.

After checking for smoke and looking carefully at the alarm, which is located right outside our bedroom door, I suddenly smiled to myself. It was Dad's not so subtle way of letting me know that while I was thinking of him, he was also there with me and he wanted me to know this somehow. That smoke alarm has never beeped since and I actually had the local firemen check it out and confirm that it is fine.

Since that day, I have felt a peace and comfort that I did not have before.

Our loved ones are with us, especially when we need them most and they will be heard...if we listen.

"Hail Mary, full of grace,
the Lord is with thee…"
—The Rosary

Joining Mary

A volunteer told me the story of how her dad died, so full of peace. Her father received a diagnosis of leukemia on a Thursday. He was a man of faith and he loved to pray the rosary. On Monday, he was out snow-blowing his and his neighbour's driveway. On Tuesday, he went into the hospital for a blood transfusion. Then things happened very quickly.

The volunteer was getting ready on Wednesday to go in to the hospital to see her father when the hospital called and said to come quickly. She hurried up, and prayed that all the family would get to the hospital on time. She called the priest, who came and gave the anointing for the sick. At about four o'clock in the afternoon, her sister and a brother from out-of-town also made it to the hospital.

Their father's eyes were always very squinty, but this time he opened his eyes really wide and indicated that there was someone there. His daughter believes it was Mary coming for him. He died at six o'clock. He did not suffer, and he was at peace.

A miracle tastes sweet
like manna in the desert.

Last Call

Another interesting story of a patient who died *twice* was told to me by a retired nurse.

It was over thirty years ago, and I remember it was a warm, sunny day. I was working in a small hospital, and caring for a lady who was near end-of-life. Suddenly, the patient stopped breathing and I called for the doctor who was in another room. He came in, listened to her heart with his stethoscope, and pronounced her dead.

At the time, I was thinking *she doesn't look dead.* Usually, I would pull the sheet up to cover the face, but this time I didn't. I also decided to wait a while before I took her to the morgue. I left the room, and a short time later, returned.

I found my dead patient out of bed and fully ambulatory! I was dumbfounded! *She was actually on the phone, talking to a relative!* Again I left the room, and when I came back in the second time, she was back in bed, dead. The other nurses were just as stunned as I was! We didn't bother calling the doctor in, because he had already pro-nounced her dead!

I will always wonder, *Who did she call, and what did she tell them?*

"Healing is possible through love,
even when a cure is not."
—Bernie Siegel

Mad at God and Everyone Else!

A friend told me this story that someone had told him. As with many stories that are told and retold, we can't be sure we have all the details straight anymore. However, this is the gist of it.

A middle-aged man was dying at home. He was a lapsed Catholic, meaning he hadn't attended church in many years. Even though he was receiving home nursing services and the best care of his devoted wife, he was very angry. Well, he knew he was dying; didn't he have a right to be angry? This fellow, however, was angry, irritable, disagreeable, and downright mean.

Eventually, someone suggested to him they might call the priest. He muttered some obscenities, kicked them out and threw something at the door. The priest got wind of it, and being a younger man, didn't know the sick fellow personally. He decided to pay a visit.

He entered the house just as the sick man was evicting yet another visitor from his bedroom. The priest took a breath and stepped into the room. When he saw the white collar, the sick man started in, "Who called you? I didn't call for a priest! What, am I dying or something?"

The young priest very wisely sat down beside the bed, not saying a word. When he felt the sick man was losing steam, he said, "I don't blame you for being angry. I'd be angry too if I were in your shoes. I don't think God blames you for being angry. In fact, He doesn't even mind if you're mad at Him."

He let that sink in awhile. "Do you think you're mad at God?" he asked.

"Darn right I am," said the sick man.

"Well, let's tell Him—He can take it; His shoulders are wide enough."

Together, for the next several minutes, they both ranted and railed at God. The man's wife wondered what was going on in that room with all the commotion.

Eventually, the priest softened his tone and prayed an earnest prayer recognizing disappointment, longing and loss. He asked for God's love to surround the man and help him walk through his illness. He asked God to absorb the man's anger. He asked for help to calm fears and worries.

The sick man lay quiet and spent. His emotions were still intense, but now different. As the priest got up to leave, the sick man held out his hand and said, *"Thank you, Father, for coming."*

Each individual soul is a
sacred creative act of God.

Mom-in-Law

My mother-in-law died in 1989. At that time, palliative care was a fairly new field of medicine. I didn't know that years later it would be my field of work.

I remember the hospital doctor and social worker gathering the family together to tell us she was dying. They took time answering our questions, and seemed genuinely sorry this was happening. In our shock, we went to the chapel, where we released the raw edges of our grief. We needed to talk, to cry and to process our feelings. Mom was in the ICU, and the nursing staff coordinated our visits in to see her, one at a time, and gently told us when it had been enough for a while.

Mom was a sweet, gentle lady, and I felt our easy relationship had more to do with her nature than mine. When it was my turn, I remember going in alone to see her in the ICU bed and saying *goodbye*. I told her that she had been a good mother-in-law. It seemed the natural thing to do.

FINAL SCENES

When they moved her to a private room, the staff knew her time was drawing near. I thought they were just being especially kind to give us the opportunity to gather around her bed-side. Did they do this for all patients, or just for our Mom? Family members kept an around-the-clock vigil. Mom died on the day after her birthday, with lots of love surrounding her. She is still missed.

A mother's love transcends
life and death…

My Obit

Have you thought about what you would like to have written on your gravestone? I know some of you have already made your funeral arrangements and have possibly considered this question. I would like to have engraved on mine, "I told you I was sick!" All jesting aside—If you were to think for a moment about what you would like others to say about you when you die, what would you come up with?

My pastoral care class found this a difficult question. It was easy to think of things to say about someone else, but not so easy to describe themselves. What qualities would they like to be remembered for? What would be a suitable epitaph?

I told them to remember that they are a *human being*, not a *human doing*. They might want to be remembered for who they were, not for what they did. I thought about my epitaph, and came up with this: "She will be remembered as someone who loved to laugh, loved people and loved life." What is it that makes you, *you*?

Why do we seek explanations
for every reality?

"No Patty-Fingers in the Holy Water..."

One of our favourite movies is *The Quiet Man*, a beautiful Irish story featuring John Wayne and Maureen O'Hara. We have seen it so many times we have memorized some of the dialogue. One of my favourite lines is spoken by the little Barry Fitzgerald: "No patty-fingers in the Holy water if you please." Every time I see the little bowl of Holy water in the chapel, a smile comes to my face and I can't help thinking about that line in the movie.

We have had quite a time with the Holy water this past winter. If you dipped your fingers in the bowl expecting them to be wet, you would be surprised to pull out a small piece of paper that said, "Due to the risk of H1N1, we are sorry to have removed the Holy water temporarily."

We have had our challenges at the hospital these past few years—starting with SARS, then Norwalk virus, Avian flu and more recently Swine flu. We are being very vigilant to take infection control precautions.

One of the Roman Catholic volunteers commented that if it is indeed Holy water, then wouldn't it be purified by God? Indeed, that sounds quite reasonable to me, and I didn't have a good answer.

As soon as the immediate scare was over, we were able to put back in the little bowl water that had been blessed by the priest. So from time to time, I put my little patty-fingers in the water in order to receive the blessing.

(Barry Fitzgerald also says in the movie: "Impetuous! Homeric!..." I'm not really sure what that means, but it sounds like fun to me.)

"Parting is such sweet sorrow..."
—William Shakespeare

Not Ready to Say Goodbye

Dr. Elisabeth Kubler-Ross has done wonderful work studying grief reactions to loss and bad news. According to her, the stages of grief are DABDA: denial, anger, bargaining, depression and acceptance. Today, we call these *possible grief reactions.* They are all valid terms, but we just don't expect that they may come in such orderly fashion. I was reminded of this lesson one day.

We had a dear, beloved friend who was an old, retired minister. We visited him often and he was a surrogate Grandpa to our kids. As he became older and frailer, his sons added his name to the long-term care lists in another part of the province.

One day, we found out quite by accident that his name had come up and he was being transferred out of town by air ambulance in two days! The news hit us hard, and I started into Kubler-Ross' five stages of grief.

A quick visit to say goodbye was organized, and I remember being pushed from denial to anger very quickly.

After he left town, I knew I might never see this friend again. I remember feeling more emotional at this time than I did some months later when we heard of his death. I rounded the corner into depression and ran down the home stretch straight toward acceptance. I was happy to have been part of his life.

One can do small things with big love.

One Starfish

There are days when I come home from my work in Spiritual Care at the hospital wishing that I had spent more time with patients and families. There are so many needs—always sick folk with fears and worries to help. There is a *revolving door* in hospital work—as soon as one goes out, another comes in. The work is never done. It puts me in mind of the story of the little boy on the beach.

The waves had brought many, many starfish up and deposited them on the beach. The boy was busy picking them up and putting them back in the water. Along came a man who commented to him that he would never be able to finish getting them *all* back in the ocean. "Well," said the little boy, looking down at the one in his hand, "I think it makes a difference to *this* one."

When I think of that boy's attitude, it boosts mine. Perhaps I have made some small difference to someone who was sick today. And hopefully, with God's help, it made a difference to *that* one.

Mother Teresa remained calm among the chaos of the sick and dying in Calcutta. How did she manage to feel at peace when she could only care for some of the many who needed her? Perhaps she, too, was able to focus, in the moment, on just the one she was caring for at the time. In her work she certainly *made a difference* to many.

If a cat has nine lives,
that's a lot of funerals!

Oscar the Cat

I love the story about how a cat was an important part of the health team. Perhaps you have read about Oscar, as he has been made famous in the news. Dr. David Dosa, who also worked on Oscar's team, wrote about him in the *New England Journal of Medicine*, and validated this story.

Oscar lives in a nursing home in Rhode Island, where many of the residents have dementia. He has an uncanny ability to detect when a resident is nearing death. No one knows exactly how or why, but Oscar can sense when a resident is nearing the last hours of life. He pads down the hall to their room, climbs up on the bed and curls up near the dying person!

He has been successful in predicting approaching death in many cases. The health team pays attention to Oscar's actions, and when they see him spending extra time with a resident, they take notice. They call the family to let them know their loved one is passing away.

They feel Oscar provides comfort and solace, and that companionship is very much appreciated. The local hospice has given him his own wall plaque, so that he knows he is a valuable part of the health team. It reads, "For his compassionate hospice care, this plaque is awarded to Oscar the Cat."

One time, a mother and her child were visiting an elderly woman who was bedridden. Oscar came in the room and climbed up next to the lady. "Why is Oscar here?" the little boy asked.

His mom answered, "He's here to help Grandma get to heaven."

"O Death, where is your sting?"
—1 Corinthians 15:55

Passing Over to Heaven

A friend told me that this experience had happened to her friend. I hope I can explain it justly. Visualize this scene. Linda's Mom was dying. She had been a widow for many years, and Linda was her only child. They were very close.

Linda was experiencing that roller-coaster ride of emotion that often accompanies the journey of illness. She was losing her Mom, and also her best friend. Many hours were spent at the bedside, that time of vigil when one cannot predict the next five minutes, let alone the next day. It is a time of waiting, of restlessness and of grief.

Finally, the doctor gently told Linda that her Mom could go at any minute; in fact, she just didn't know why her mom was still hanging on. "Perhaps you can tell her that it's all right to let go," she suggested. Sometimes the dying person needs to know that family members are going to be all right. Sometimes, they just need that permission to die. So after hearing this advice, this is what Linda did.

93

She got up onto the bed and gathered her Mom in her arms. She told her that she loved her and would miss her, but that she would be all right. She told her that it was all right to let go and die.

Then she did something extraordinary. She said, "I'm going to walk with you, Mom, until you die. You will be safe and with Dad." Slowly, she described the journey, the ascending path and the glow of light. She told her that they were going higher and higher and the light was getting stronger now. She said she could feel the love and asked her Mom if she could feel it, too. There was no reply so she continued on.

"Mom, look," she said, "I can see Dad. He's coming to get you. Can you see him?" Again, there was no reply. "Dad is so happy to see you. I can't go with you, but I am going to put your hand in Dad's and then you will be safe."

Tears were falling down Linda's face by this time. Then she took her Mom's hand out of her right hand and transferred it over to her left hand. "I'm going now, Mom," she said, "I love you, and goodbye."

Linda let go of her mom and sat back, spent and quietly weeping in the chair. Her mom died. Linda had walked with her mom *to the gates of heaven.*

Laughter is cheap, easy
and a readily available medicine!

Patch Adams

Last fall, my husband and I had the pleasure of hearing Patch Adams speak at Queen's University. This is the real Dr. Patch Adams, the clown, doctor and social advocate! The auditorium was packed with medical students as he described his work all over the world with the Gesundheit Institute.

Patch is sincerely warm and friendly, refreshingly funny, and also brilliant. He is a man who says he only made seventeen pages of notes all through medical school! He has three thousand books in his house. He thrives on almost no sleep and he has energy and enthusiasm for all people and their problems. His medical missions all over the world attract thousands who beg to go with him and be part of his ministry.

Although he does not profess to be a Christian, he says that when we do this kind of work, we are heroes—*we are acting as Christ to one another!* He also gives his Mother total credit for his worldview.

He taught us seven points to being this kind of hero:

1. Love people. (Patch especially loves the poor, the mentally ill and the physically impaired.)
2. Recognize that you *are a hero* when you do small acts of kindness to others. Love yourself so that you can love others.
3. The primary job in caring is to LOVE. Love heals many hurts.
4. Be JESUS to one another.
5. Be creative in handling problems.
6. Be enthusiastic. It is contagious.
7. At the end of it all, caring is good for you! You essentially get more out of it than you put in.

In jotting down these points of wisdom, I recognized that these are directions to providing Christian pastoral care. May God bless Patch Adams, because he is clearly doing God's work!

*"May the Lord bless you
and keep you…"*
—The Aaronic Blessing

Praying the Rosary

Whenever a volunteer tells me that she is *just a volunteer,* I am quick to correct her. There is no such thing as *just a volunteer,* I say. "You are a valuable part of the team and we could not get along without you!"

There are a variety of duties filled by spiritual care volunteers, and we try to find the right one for each individual. There is a volunteer who makes tiny cards with a single Bible verse on each one: *"…casting all your care upon Him, for He cares for you"* (1 Peter 5:7).

This volunteer made me chuckle, because I sent her in to play cards with a fellow, and when she arrived on the floor, the fellow had been moved. She didn't play cards anyway, but that didn't stop her from putting her time to good use! She asked the nurse which patient might appreciate a visit, and then sat down to a game of *Snakes and Ladders!* Later, she asked me in jest if playing *Snakes and Ladders* was part of her spiritual care volunteer job description! (I guess being flexible comes in the small print: *Other duties as assigned!*)

There is a volunteer who changes the worship service board each month, and another who makes sure the chapel is tidy. Some volunteers come in specifically to push wheelchairs so patients can come to weekly worship services.

Each task is appreciated and fits together to form a comprehensive spiritual care service. One dear volunteer, a little lady, does something no one else does. She comes in regularly to sit in chapel and pray for the patients. You can sometimes find her in chapel, all alone, very quietly praying the rosary. I smile when I think of her. What a valuable gift she offers—the prayers of a loving heart. Thanks be to God!

Sometimes we do not receive
our rewards in this life.
—Hebrews 11:13, paraphrased

Pulling the Plug

You have heard this term before. When a person's body is being kept on life support, there may be difficult decisions to be made. I don't know how many times I have heard a family member refer to withdrawing life support as *pulling the plug.* The image that comes to my mind is a distressing one. I actually picture a very upset family member pulling an electric plug to stop a machine, and the patient immediately dying. Wow. What baggage would that act leave on a loving daughter or son?

A few weeks ago, a volunteer chaplain told the story of being called in to hospital in the middle of the night to help a distressed family. Their mother had just had a massive stroke, and was on life support. The family members were in shock, confusion and distress. The siblings, all having different personalities, were having trouble discussing the inevitable, and their emotions were all over the map.

When the chaplain came in to the room, they were arguing about *pulling the plug.* He stayed, listened, provided comfort and gave them time to begin to process their feelings. Toward morning, he felt they were ready to discuss withdrawal of treatment. He had to emphasize that the mother was dying *because of her illness*, not because of any action the children had taken to withdraw life support.

Never use the term *pulling the plug.* It only serves to leave guilt. If a person felt he was responsible for *pulling the plug,* then he might feel responsible for someone's death. Choosing to withdraw treatment is a natural and ethical decision for someone holding power of attorney for personal care, *if it is in line with what the patient would have chosen for himself.* We must be careful in our use of terminology. We do not want to add anything to one's burden of grief.

"If I can't go to doggie heaven,
then I'm not going!"
—Aunt Carrie

Releasing a Burden

I looked at the list of patients who had requested visits from spiritual care, and, as always, tried to determine which one I would start with. Sometimes there is no rhyme or reason to it—you just go with your gut feeling—or the *Spirit's* leading. So I chose to visit Lillian.

Lillian had come into the hospital in severe pain, and she was being assessed and closely monitored. Her condition must have been palliative, because the palliative care nurse was just leaving as I was entering the room.

Sometimes I think it helps not to read the patient's chart ahead of time. I can go in with a blank slate and let the patient take me where she needs to go. Undoubtedly, Lillian was having serious physical pain, and that was being tended to. It soon became apparent this little lady had a great deal of spiritual and emotional pain, too. As soon as introductions and niceties were completed, Lillian burst into tears. What she was most troubled about was her little dog. So many times this is the case. Lillian had no children or husband, and her closest friend was a little toy poodle named Rocky. She was missing Rocky so much, and was hoping that he was being well cared for by the neighbours while she was in hospital.

I assured her that if she had to stay in hospital any length of time, we would see to it that Rocky got in to visit her. That seemed to help somewhat—but there was more, and many more tears. Lillian told me a sad story of being hurt very badly by her Father when her Mother died in 1969. I quickly did the math—that was 41 years ago! Evidently, at the funeral, in a state of acute grief, he had told Lillian that she was responsible for her Mother dying of cancer. I was stunned. How very painful, to have guilt added to grief. Their relationship had been estranged from that point on. The Father had long since died.

I'm no counselor, but I believe God led me in what I did next.

I put my hands on her face and told her I loved her. Then, as she held both my hands so tightly, I told her about how Jesus loves her, always and forever. Then I told her that God will be her Father and has been all along. Then I prayed a simple, earnest prayer for healing for all the past hurts and memories. There were more tears. I prayed for a release of a burden, and when we were finished, I smiled at her. "Do you believe God wants this healing for you?" I asked. Finally, she nodded. "Then you must believe He has given it to you," I said. Just then, the Doctor came in, and as I left, they were discussing medications.

I saw Lillian in a wheelchair in the lobby later that day as I was on my way home. Some friends were visiting her; perhaps they were the ones who were looking after Rocky. I spoke to her and she held out her hand to touch mine. "Thank you," she said.

"Make a joyful shout to the Lord..."
—Psalm 100:1

Singing for Company

The first time I provided hospice care, it was informally arranged by my ladies' Bible study group. I had just met this pretty woman in her mid-thirties, and I was told she had breast cancer. "That's a wig she's wearing, you know", I was told. No, I didn't know. I was surprised that she was failing so quickly, and we were told her condition was palliative.

Our group mobilized to help with the many practical needs of caring for her at home. She had three children and a husband who was beside himself with anxiety. I felt like an outsider, as I had never been to her home before, but I wanted to help in some small way. I was scheduled to sit at her bedside, to keep her company and to read to her from her Bible. It was quite an enjoyable visit and I did most of the talking, as I recognized she was too weak to participate.

She asked me to sing some simple praise choruses. I remember thinking that I guess I can do that, and sang a few easy pieces, such as *Jesus loves me* and *Jesus bids us shine.* I said goodbye and came down the stairs. Company had come in the back door. It was then I noticed a baby monitor on the kitchen counter. It was used to communicate with Mom up in her bedroom. My face turned beet red as I realized they had just heard my little concert over the speaker! I left and realized that allowing myself to be vulnerable was the gift I brought to the bedside that day.

What if we could "beam 'em up" to
Heaven without dying first?

Star Trek, Please

Gary had come to the hospital, having recently experienced muscle failure in his legs, and was waiting for placement. We call such waiting cases ALC—*Alternative level of
care*—meaning that the hospital is not the best place for
such patients, and *placement* usually means a transfer to
long-term care.

Gary had been told he had a chronic degenerating illness, and a wheelchair would be his new reality. When I
met him, he was just mulling this over in his mind. He did a
great deal of *mulling* over the next few weeks I visited him.

He was having a difficult time getting his head around
the ideas of being in a wheelchair and a nursing home. You
see, Gary was only forty-seven. He was younger than me. I
hardly knew what to say to provide any sense of comfort.
It was not a time for platitudes or pat answers. His best
days had already gone by and his dreams for the future
were markedly changed.

I asked him what he enjoyed doing in his spare time. Suddenly, he became animated as he described science fiction—*Star Wars* and *Star Trek*. He was a *Trekkie!*

I told him I would try to find him some movies and books to enjoy. When I asked the recreation therapist, he shook his head slowly, and said he was sorry. There were no such resources, as "this is not the demographic we usually serve." I decided I would look at home, as our son loved sci-fi and he may have left some of his books and movies behind when he left home.

Over the next month or so, I visited Gary and brought him movies and books. He appreciated having something enjoyable to pass the time. One afternoon, I went up to his room with a new book, and he told me he was leaving the next day. His third-choice nursing home had a bed for him. I asked him how he felt about the move, and he told me of his difficult adjustment coming to the hospital from home. Then he said he was finally getting used to the hospital; the staff was nice to him and he was sort of settling in. Now he had to start over, in a new place and in a new town. I prayed with him, as always, and we said our goodbyes. I walked away feeling incredibly unsettled. I still get this feeling whenever I think of Gary. I know God has his plan for Gary. I sure wish I knew what it was. I sure wish Gary knew what it was.

*Whatever provides the patient
comfort is good hospice care.*

"Thanks, Sister."

I was called to the palliative care unit to visit Jean-Michel. He was a French-Canadian, a retired concierge of a large hotel, and was nearing end-of-life. He was very sick, but he had a great smile. He spoke in quite a strong French accent, but we had no trouble understanding each other. I would have switched to my poor conversational French if needed. I don't remember the details of how he came to be in our town or if he had family nearby.

I held his hand while we talked, and we prayed together familiar words of comfort, the *Our Father*. Knowing I might not see him again, I gave him the Aaronic Blessing. At the end of our visit, I turned to leave. He said, "Thanks, Sister." I left feeling strangely blessed. I am not a nun, nor am I Roman Catholic. However, if he felt I acted as a nun toward him—if I acted for him as someone he trusted and respected in his faith tradition—then I was honoured to be filling that role. No corrections needed.

God can mend a broken heart, but we
have to give Him all the pieces.

The Book of Instructions

Often, the distress of a dying person is more about worrying for loved ones than for oneself. For example, a mother may worry more about how her husband and children are going to cope without her than she would about her own level of pain control. One particular case illustrated this concept beautifully.

A couple had been married many years. They had no children. All their married life, they had taken care of each other, and in the old-fashioned, gender-specific roles. The wife did the *wifely* things and the husband did the *husbandly* things. The wife was now dying.

The palliative care nurses working with her soon found out that she was very concerned about how her husband was going to look after things when she was gone. But she had a plan! She was taking every available opportunity to work on her *Book of Instructions*. She was hand-writing a notebook full of instructions on how to do all the *wifely* things. She explained how to work the oven, how to run the washing machine, and how to wash the clothes! She left his favourite recipes and tips on how to do the grocery shopping. In fact, this task was so important that the lady said she was not going to die until it was all finished!

Eventually, she handed the little notebook over to the nurses, and died. As per her wishes, they presented it to her husband. I truly hope that she is looking down on him from heaven, and giving him encouragement and advice as he takes on his new role. May he be consoled in his grief by her handwriting.

*"We are not human beings going
through a temporary spiritual
experience, we are spiritual beings
going through a temporary
human experience."*
—Author Unknown

The Day I Should Stop Nursing

A young nurse of eighteen had just finished her training and was assigned to the pediatric ward in a large hospital. She performed her duties very carefully, and with love, as she took very seriously the responsibility of caring for such young, vulnerable lives.

One of her patients was a little boy about four years-old. He was very sick with cancer. He charmed everyone who came into his room, and the young nurse was smitten with him. His laughter was contagious.

The child got sicker, and the nurse cared for him through the night, but by morning the little fellow died. The nurse did what she had to do—attended the body, straightened the room and did up the chart. Then she left and went into the linen closet and shut the door. She let the tears come, and they overwhelmed her in great sobs.

Her nursing supervisor came in and found her crying, and told her, "Get your act together; if you are going to be any kind of a nurse, you are going to have to keep yourself from falling apart every time you lose a patient!"

The young nurse had red hair, and her passionate emotion changed to one of defiance. She responded, "The day that the death of a person does not affect me is the day that I should stop nursing."

That young nurse just retired from a full career of nursing, ending her years as a pediatric palliative care case manager. She is now enjoying retirement, and in her spare time provides hospice training to volunteers!

"Hope springs eternal..."
—Alexander Pope

The Hope Chest

Listen to this tale of one friend's love for another:

After losing Jaclyn, my best friend and confidante, it took me some time to accept that she was really gone. I became even closer with her daughter, Angelica, which helped us both. Angelica was pregnant with her first child when her Mom died. Jaclyn never got to hold *peanut,* as she referred to the unborn child.

Angelica knew that her Mom and I were *soul mate* friends, and that our family had been a part of her life for many years. It seemed normal that she would reach out to me during the loss of her beautiful and special Mom. I hoped that in some way I could bring comfort to her. Obviously, I could never replace her Mom, but I had a strong desire to be there when and if she needed me. I knew that Jaclyn would be pleased.

The birth of Angelica's first son was a joyous occasion, mixed with a touch of poignancy because her Mom was not there to share her joy. Nothing can replace your Mother at such a special moment.

Time passed, and Angelica had a second son, and life was good. However, she still missed her Mom terribly and looked for signs of her presence. She was often rewarded with a mourning dove that would suddenly appear at her window. Sometimes she dreamt that her Mom came to the door for tea, and they would sit and chat at her kitchen table as they had often done over the years. These were Angelica's favourite dreams.

One night, I had a dream. I dreamt that Jaclyn and I were looking at her *hope chest.* Jaclyn was very excited, showing me all the treasures that she had been collecting since she was sixteen years-old. Jaclyn had shown me this *hope chest,* and I could tell that it was very special to her. When I woke up, I suddenly remembered the hope chest.

That night I called Angelica and asked if she had ever seen the *hope chest* among her mother's things. She hadn't. I told her that it must be somewhere, because Jaclyn came to me in a dream to remind me of it.

Angelica was visiting her family home a week or two later and did some investigating on her own, and unbelievably, in the crawl space under the stairs, there it was! It was a beautiful mahogany chest, full of Jaclyn's treasures. Inside was her wedding dress, drawings that her three children had done over the years and special keepsakes and cards. Though tears filled her eyes, Angelica was filled with joy. The treasures inside had changed since Jaclyn was sixteen years old. Now it held all that was dear and special to her.

I don't know why Jaclyn chose that particular time to come to me in a dream, but I felt very privileged that Jaclyn had chosen me to convey this special message. The hope chest must have been very important to her, and she wanted her daughter to know it was there. In life we were always there for one another, and I was overjoyed to be of help to her still.

A Mother's love never ends...not even after death.

"...that those who do not see may
see..."
—John 9:39

The Light Bulb Went On!

If you have never been told about death, or experienced it first-hand, I imagine you might be much like a child. We all know the mistaken assumptions children make, and the questions they ask. We are careful not to tell a child that Grandpa is *sleeping*, or Grandma has *passed*, for obvious reasons.

The office volunteer told me about her developmentally-challenged cousin, Marla. The family had always protected her from funerals, as they didn't want her upset, so they thought she didn't really understand all that happened surrounding death.

Marla went into hospital, very sick with a systemic infection. When gangrene set in, the doctors had to amputate her leg. This is most distressing for someone who has limited understanding. In fact, it would be most distressing for anyone. During these days, Marla told the family that "She wanted to go home." She said this often—in fact, she

116

said it daily for more than a month. It was always, "I want to go home."

She was always told, "I'm sorry, you can't go home."

When her other leg became gangrenous as well, the Doctor told the family that he just didn't feel her heart would stand the surgery. Marla was too sick, and already on a morphine pump for pain.

Again, she asked to go home. Finally, the volunteer said, it was like *the light bulb went on!* Marla must be talking about a different home, not her earthly home! She needed permission to *go,* and without realizing it, everyone had been withholding it!

The volunteer went to her cousin and said, "I am so sorry, Marla. I didn't understand. Of course you can *go home*." She named all the family members who were already in heaven. Marla had the permission she was waiting for, and died within the hour. She finally went *home*.

"There'll be no locks or bolts between
us, Mary Kate—except those in your
own mercenary little heart!"
—Sean Thornton in *The Quiet Man*

The Locked Gates

Hear this story from a faithful daughter:

Mother died from a massive stroke at the long-term care home where she had lived for the last years of her life. She was bright and intelligent until the end, and was constantly teasing the workers in the home. They just loved her. Unfortunately, she was deaf and suffering from macular degeneration, and was going blind as well. She dreaded that thought and said she might as well be a *vegetable*.

Sometimes I would drive to the city to meet my sister and best friend, and have a visit with Mom. They were never long visits, but always enjoyable. Sometimes, we took her out to her favourite restaurant, and she would sing songs at the table. My sister and I would just sing along because it made her happy.

It was difficult for her to get around, as she had broken her hip and was in a wheel chair. Though it was unwieldy to transfer her, we managed and she always had fun. This happened three or four times a year.

I always had the feeling that Mom wanted me to stay longer for a visit, but with small kids at home, working full time and a house and husband to look after, I never seemed to have enough time for anything. It was something I never felt good about, but it was just the way it was at that time.

After Mom died, my husband and I drove to where she was buried beside her husband in a beautiful cemetery. When we got there, it was around 4:30 p.m. and we drove through the gates and found the spot fairly quickly. I said a prayer, kissed the stone monument and we got back in the car to leave.

Suddenly, we noticed that the gates were closed and locked. *Okay*...so we drove to the next set of gates. They were locked, too! Little did we know that all of the cemetery gates are locked at 5:00 p.m. sharp!

We were pondering what to do, and I must admit, were feeling slightly anxious at being locked in a cemetery. After driving around for what seemed like a very long time, we did find an escape route at the very end of the cemetery property. By then it was close to 6:00 p.m. Needless to say, we were quite relieved and laughed nervously.

It occurred to me that my Mom had decided that this was one time when she would ensure that we stayed a bit longer than we planned. My husband and I chuckled, because it would be the kind of humour my Mom would enjoy.

Never underestimate the power of a Mom, even after death.

*"I keep a close watch on this heart
of mine; I keep my eyes wide
open all the time."*
—Johnny Cash, "Walk the Line"

The Narrow Lane

An older retired farmer told me this story about his brother. When he was a young man, he tried to live the Christian life, but for some reason he was always falling away. *He fell off the path,* is how he put it. When he was only twenty-nine, and married, he suffered a heart attack. He was taken to hospital, and was being prepped for emergency surgery. He died on the operating table.

He was clinically dead for about ten minutes. Suddenly, his hand moved! It made the doctor jump. He woke up and told the story of dying and going to heaven. He had met Jesus, who was dressed in white robes. Jesus told him, "If you will serve me, I will let you return to earth." The young man promised that he would, and came back to life as a changed man. He lived his whole life, following the *narrow line,* and died the second time, as an old man, of a heart attack.

I know what I know, beyond the shadow
of a doubt, because I know in my spirit.

The Spirit Knows

I have often wondered how the spirit can sense something
that the conscious mind cannot. Why do we sometimes
get a sense of something, an intuition or a feeling? Is it because our spirit knows and feels things that we cannot understand? I have accepted this lack of human understanding as the mystery surrounding the spirit. Sometimes, *the
spirit just knows.*

One of our hospice volunteers has a very keen sense of
spirituality. This spiritual nature follows her in her hospital
visits. She had been visiting a male patient in hospital for a
long time, and they had developed a bond. After her regular Tuesday visit, the man got out of bed, shook her hand
and said "Goodbye."

On Saturday, the volunteer found herself in the inten-
sive care unit with her Mother who was sick with a heart
condition. As she was waiting in the hallway, something
told her to go up onto the floor to visit her male patient.
At this point, he was in a coma. He died the following day.

His spirit had known he was dying, because he had said his goodbyes on Tuesday, on their last regular visit together.

Another spiritual moment came at the bedside, as she prayed for a patient who had been declared *brain-dead*. As she prayed, the volunteer could see the body changing. She said it was hard to describe, but she felt the patient's spirit was still alive, and acknowledging the prayer. She felt the spirit was not yet ready to leave the body, but welcomed the prayers.

Scientists have done tests to determine the moment the spirit leaves the body. They can measure the energy as it lifts and disperses after the moment of death. On the other hand, I prefer the less scientific practice one nurse has, of opening a window when her patient has died, *to let the Spirit go free*.

When Christ comes calling,
I will gladly go with Him.

The Uncles

This story is about the family of a hospice volunteer.

Mother had four brothers. They happened to die in reverse order—from youngest to oldest. Her three-year-old brother was sick and dying in England of pneumonia. Before he died, he described a man standing at the foot of his bed. He said the man had long hair and a beard, and wanted him to go with him. The boy said, "Tell the man to go away. I don't want to go." After the child died, the family wondered if the person at the end of the bed had been his grandfather, who had already died—or, perhaps he was Christ, calling him home.

When the oldest brother, the last one to die, was very sick at Christmastime, he saw a strange apparition. Family members were gathered around the foot of the bed. There was a gap in the line. This brother described seeing his own son filling in the gap. He had died a few years before. This gave him the comfort of knowing he would soon be with those who had gone before him. He died a few months later.

A kindred spirit is worth
more than silver and gold.

The Wounded Healer

Henri Nouwen, a famous theologian, priest and professor, wrote the book called *The Wounded Healer.* He speaks about the pastoral caregiver as a *wounded soul*, approaching the bedside in order to minister to another wounded soul. He says that we, the caregivers, are not perfect. We come to provide care as wounded souls, with all of our bumps and blemishes. It is because we are not perfect, or do not have our own act totally together, that we can reach out to the injured soul of another.

Pastoral care is all about human souls connecting. I believe this is a key element in healing. That is why, I believe, we do not have robots nursing our patients!

I coordinate, train and support the work of the pastoral care volunteers in the hospital. They are an assorted group of people, and I love each one. One is very hard of hearing; another has failed eyesight; one walks only with a cane; another is too frail to push a wheelchair; one does her visiting as it fits in alongside her schedule of many doctor's appointments and therapies; another just lost her husband, but visits to give someone else a lift. Yet another volunteer was abused as a child, and is still going for therapy.

I am always very thankful for my "wounded healers." I am proud of their courage, strength, sense of purpose and their love for one another. It is in helping others heal that they too find healing. There are gifts to be found in providing spiritual care!

It is a blessing to be
child-like in our faith.

"There's a Piece of
Paper on My Tongue"

I have always felt that Holy Communion is very sacred. We offer a Roman Catholic communion, an Anglican Eucharist and a Protestant communion at the hospital. I hope that covers all the bases! As an ecumenical chaplain, I believe God accepts our sacrament of communion regardless of the creed or liturgy from which it comes.

I also believe God has a sense of humour, because a few funny things have happened during communion service at the hospital! You know how the minister is always prepared for a surprising response when he asks the children a question during story time in church service? Well, it is very similar working with patients suffering from dementia. You just don't know what they will come out with sometimes!

The Anglican Priest was serving the *bread*, which is a little hard wafer. When he came to a little lady with Alzheimer's, he placed it on her tongue. She must have remembered the *bread* as a soft square cut from a piece of bread like the United and Presbyterians use. In astonishment, she said out loud, "He put a piece of paper on my tongue!"

Everyone smiled and someone assured her it was okay to swallow it. Because she has no short-term memory, it happened again just the other day! "That's just a piece of paper!" she said, when again served communion. Again, we all smiled.

The priest continued serving communion, and then noticed a gentleman outside in the hall. He stepped out and offered communion to him, too. This particular fellow is always very chatty and rather loud, and proceeded to tell the priest his latest joke about *meals on wheels!* The priest very patiently waited for the punch line, then patted the gentleman's shoulder and made his way back to continue the service. I just love how the priest is able to exhibit grace and understanding and just go with the flow.

Take my body,
but not my soul.

Throw It Off the
Almonte Bridge!

Many years ago, my husband and I paid a visit to Mable, a retired friend who was sick and had moved in with her daughter. We knew she was sick, but we just didn't know how sick. Did she have cancer? Was she going to die? It was a time when the *C-word* wasn't used freely—a time when having a diagnosis of cancer was just about the same as being given a death sentence.

When we asked Mable how she was, she said, "Some tests are good, and some are not so good." We could see Mable was wearing a wig, which meant, I guess, that she was getting chemotherapy.

Suddenly, out of the blue, Mable pulled off her wig, waved it in the air, and said, "I would just like to throw this off the Almonte bridge!" We were speechless. We looked at our friend, now bald, and hadn't a clue what to say. I did not know then that my life's work would take a path leading to end-of-life care. Little did I know that years later, I would be teaching others about what to say in such a situation.

The operation was a success,
but the patient died.

Throwing Up in the Supermarket

The mind is a very complex machine. I am often amazed at how the mind works. In fact, I don't really understand it at all. There is a *remembered response* mechanism, which allows the mind to remember and pull out information that is not in our conscious memory.

An example of this is when I absent-mindedly am eating an apple, and I put it down; the unconscious mind knows I haven't finished eating that apple, and directs my conscious mind to go looking for it. Another example is when the radio in the car is turned down so low I cannot hear it, but I begin humming a tune, and when I turn up the volume I am right in step with the song being played. Maybe this is just me—maybe this doesn't work with you at all!

Anyway, I want to tell you about a cancer patient who had a subconscious learned response. A man in his early twenties was going to the cancer centre for a very treatable form of cancer, and after a grueling regimen of che-

131

motherapy, he was again well. The cancer centre nurse told me this story.

One day, about two years after she had last seen the fellow, she ran into him in a supermarket. She wouldn't even have paid any attention to him, except that when he rounded the corner with his grocery cart and saw her, immediately he started to projectile vomit! He was very embarrassed, and apologized to her profusely. She was bewildered, and knew she wasn't that bad-looking, so what could have been the cause of such a violent reaction?!

Then he told her that he had been her patient. Just seeing her again reminded him of his cancer treatment. That reminded him of the chemotherapy. That reminded him of the nausea and vomiting. All these reactions occurred in mere seconds.

He told her he had the same reaction of extreme nausea whenever he passed the cancer centre, and threw up if he had to stop at the stoplight. He had learned to take a different route to avoid it. Then he told her what a wonderful nurse she had been—his favourite one. He said goodbye and hoped he would never see her again! Incredibly, that left her feeling somewhat better!

*"When you wish upon a star; Makes no
difference who you are; Anything your
heart desires—Will come to you"*
—Louis Armstrong

Two Wishes

Nathan William Chedore died in 1999, when he was almost nineteen years old. He died from congestive heart failure, a result of Duchene Muscular Dystrophy. Although he was ill for most of his childhood, he had a tremendous spirit. Nathan used to say that everyone needed to laugh ten times and give six hugs each day.

Toward the end of his short life, Nathan expressed that there were two things he wished for: he wanted to *be famous* and he wanted to *fall in love*. Nathan wanted someone to love him back—someone who wasn't family and who wasn't being paid to care for him.

This is how he became "famous." His mother, Terri, had become very good friends with Nathan's case manager, Jan. After Nathan died, they prepared an educational slide presentation on pediatric palliative care, using Nathan's case. It was called *Nathan's Story*. Together, they presented it more than a dozen times locally—for the community hospice, the medical staff and chaplaincy care team at the hospital, local women's groups, in a city high school, to a nursing alumni association, a one-parent family association and to a pastoral care program.

Terri and Jan also presented it for the pediatric nurses at the Children's Hospital of Eastern Ontario. The highlight was presenting at the Canadian Hospice-Palliative Care conference in Victoria, BC, in 2001. Nathan's story has touched many, many health professionals and caregivers. 1,000 bookmarks with Nathan's picture were given out.

Nathan has had three sections of the Trans-Canada Trail dedicated in honour of him—one in Ottawa, one in Campbellton, New Brunswick, and one in Moncton, New Brunswick. A hand-carved bench was crafted by Terri's brother and sits along the trail in one of the locations.

Nathan's life has been well-remembered!

Now for the love story! Nathan had a hospice volunteer visit regularly. In the course of conversation, he found out she had a daughter with a very unusual name. He told her he used to know a girl by that name in junior high, but they had lost touch. (Nathan had to drop out of school in grade eleven when he experienced heart trouble.) Was this girl her daughter? he asked.

She was reluctant to admit that it was, as she was keen on keeping a confidential relationship, but after a while Nathan wore her down, and she admitted that, yes, her daughter was the girl he used to know.

Nathan sent home a note with the hospice volunteer, and got a note from the daughter in return. Eventually, he got brave enough to phone her. After reconnecting, they became inseparable. She was often at Nathan's house, talking with him and playing video games.

Their relationship was, however, short-lived. They met in October, and Nathan died in December. They had only a few months together, but it brought them both a great deal of happiness. They were head over heels in love. One night, they shared a special romantic candlelit dinner. His Mom had prepared it according to Nathan's instructions, and then she was told to "scram!"

On the night Nathan died, his girlfriend had had to phone strangers down the road to take her to the hospital in the middle of night. She lived in the country, and it was snowing. She was the last person he spoke to.

This young woman who became the love of his short life continues to be an important part of the Chedore family. She lived with them until just recently, while attending university to obtain her Master's in Occupational Therapy.

Nathan's parents are grieving the loss of their only child. They do, however, find comfort in knowing that he had both of his final wishes come true.

"Greater love has no one than this, than
to lay down one's life for his friends."
—John 15:13

Uncle Carl

Gillian told me this story:

Uncle Carl was one of those young men who signed up to go to war a year early. He was only seventeen when he went over to England for training. I don't know many of the details, except that he was killed in the war.

Another young man from his company made it safely home. He lived in Johnstown, and Grandma and Grandpa paid him a visit, because they needed to know more information about their son's death. The soldier told him that Carl had died from a hand-grenade explosion.

Years later, I had a session with a spiritual reader. After a prayer, she asked me to give her a review of our family—like a genealogy review. I was working on my Mom's side of the family at the time, so I asked the spiritual reader if the spirit of my Uncle Carl was with me.

She said he was, so I asked her to tell me about him. She told me that Uncle Carl had been murdered. (Well, I have always felt war is *murder*.) She went on, "First he was shot in the leg, and that's what put him down. Then there was a bomb, and he blew up." She went on to tell me that Uncle Carl had not regretted dying for his country. That gave me a sense of peace. I take great pride in Uncle Carl's gift.

Whether I live, or whether I die,
my hope is in the Lord.
—Philippians 1:20, paraphrased

Waiting for a Better Day

This story of Mary I heard from Reverend Paul, preached from the pulpit in today's sermon. I assume it is true.

The minister went to the house of a man, who invited him in and took him upstairs to the bedroom. He opened a bureau drawer and took out something wrapped in tissue. It was a silk slip trimmed in intricate lace. It still had the original price tag on it, and the price was quite steep.

"This was Mary's slip," the man said, "She bought it the first time we visited Montreal. That was about eight or nine years ago. She never wore it. She was always waiting for the right occasion. Well, I guess this is it."

He took the slip from its wrappings and laid it on the pile of clothes on the bed. These are the things he had ready to take to the funeral home. "I guess that occasion is now."

After telling us the sad story of Mary, our minister told us to enjoy each moment we are given. Enjoy each occasion and each joy, and not to save our best for some far-off day. He said we should use the good china and silver to celebrate more often—celebrate finishing planting the garden or celebrate the beginning of March break.

This fits my life philosophy that I teach in end-of-life care. That quality of life is for *now*.

I have known you since I knit you
together in your mother's womb.
—Psalm 139:13, paraphrased

"Warehoused" in Nursing Homes

I received this story by email from a distressed daughter. The fact that she was a high-level health administrator who knew the health system through and through did not make her distress any easier. She described this situation of her elderly mother.

Mrs. Osborne was ninety-three years-old. She was in hospital after having surgery to repair a broken hip due to a fall. Many times, a broken hip in an elderly person can put the body into trauma, and if it is not strong enough, the organs can shut down, starting with the kidneys. What might be a major injury in a younger person sometimes proves fatal in an older patient.

When the daughter went in to see her mother for the first time, she found her heavily medicated. After a few days, Mrs. Osborne was well enough to sit up and converse. She still, of course, could not put her weight on the injured leg.

One afternoon, the charge nurse met the daughter on her way in to visit her mom. She spoke about *the next steps* for Mrs. Osborne. She suggested short-term rehab followed by admission to a nursing home.

At hearing this, the daughter was most alarmed. "Mom took care of herself," she said, "She has always managed very well. After she recovers, we fully expect her to go back home".

The nurse then said that her assessment of her mother showed confusion, mild agitation and perhaps the beginning stages of dementia. She couldn't speak clearly or put on her own clothes. Surely it would not be safe for her Mom to live on her own any more.

The daughter thought for a few moments and then she said, "Can't you give mom some more time? Give her a few more days to recover, and some rehab therapy. Although Mom was getting very slow, she could wash and dress herself and make simple meals. We helped to do the housekeeping and other chores. You need to remember a few things about my Mom. She is in a strange environment, she still has anesthetic in her system, not to mention high doses of pain-killer, and she does not have her hearing aids in, her glasses on, or her teeth in. In that situation, wouldn't you come across as being a bit confused, too?" The nurse smiled and let her go on. "Mom is a very proud and independent lady. She would lose her spirit if we put her in a nursing home. If Mom loses her spirit, then I know she will die."

They agreed to send Mrs. Osborne to a short-term rehab bed in the hospital, and to reassess her later after she was more mobile.

The daughter finished her email with a distressing question. She asked, "Why are we so in a hurry to *warehouse* our older adults." I have thought a great deal about that question.

"On the wings of a snow-white dove, He sends His pure sweet love; A sign from above… on the wings of a dove."
—Bob Fergusson

Winged Message

My name is Lynn. I lost my best friend and cousin in 2001. We had been best friends since we were sixteen, when her aunt married my dad. Of all the cousins that I met, Jacquie just stood out. I was painfully shy, and she genuinely welcomed me to the family and somehow even made me feel special. She had a very sweet nature and we soon found that we shared the same sense of humour. There was always an angelic spirituality that emanated from her.

At around eighteen years of age or so, we moved into an apartment together, and she and her fiancé introduced me to my husband. Jacquie and I shared everything—from the birth of our children to our dreams of the future and all the normal ups and downs of everyday life. We went to concerts and spent holidays together. We had many joyful times.

Every Sunday, one of us would call the other to share the week's events, usually at suppertime. It was kind of a joke between us, because we knew that our hubbies would continue cooking the dinner while we chatted. It was a kind of tiny conspiracy!

Jacquie had to have a second heart valve replacement in 2001, and we all said that at her young age she would soar through the operation. She never shared her fears with me, if she had any, about the possibility of not surviving. She would never want to worry any of us. Unfortunately, Jacquie died thirty days after her surgery, from a major blood clot to the brain. Everyone was devastated.

When I returned home the day after the funeral, I was dazed. While I was unpacking our car, I heard a blackbird cawing in the tree on our front yard. Being a lover of birds and wondering what all the din was about, I mimicked his call. I often do this when I hear a bird call.

It made me smile to think that I could be distracted by the call of a bird at such a sad moment. I kept this up for a minute or so while unpacking. Suddenly, the blackbird landed above the trunk of the car and just sat there cawing away.

At first I couldn't believe it, and called my husband to see it. He came out and the bird was still sitting on the car, cawing away. I could have reached out and touched him. It really floored us both.

Jacquie and I had always shared a love of birds, and I believe that it was Jacquie telling me—very noisily I might add, because she really wanted me to pay attention—that she is okay and that I shouldn't be so sad. There was a little humour in her method of sending the message that made me chuckle. Jacquie could always make me laugh. I never saw the bird again, but I have always felt that Jacquie is still right here with me, in my heart every day.

*Our lives on earth are but a drop in the
bucket compared to eternity.*

"You Devil, You."

I imagine there will come a day when I, too, will find my-self living in long-term care. Regardless of how many changes may occur between now and then, it will still be communal living and a great change from individual family dwelling. We no longer use the terms *facilities* or even *in-stitutions*, we now call them *long-term care homes*. Still, no getting around it, communal living is not the place of choice for many of the elderly.

Pete comes to mind. He is a tall fellow, now stooped over, who uses a walker. He has lived in the long-term care home for a long time, and has accepted that this is his real-ity. He is a real character, and it's his strength of character that I feel has been his greatest support. He walks the halls, slowly and bent over, as if he has somewhere to go. He greets everyone in a big, loud voice—he's hard of hear-ing too—and he always has a story. His only hobby that I have ever observed is that every day when the newspaper comes round, Pete shakes it until the page with the *Jumble* comes out. He plays the word game for as long as it takes to finish it. This routine of Pete's has been his life for, well, I don't know how long.

Quite regularly, I will pass by Pete, and he will look up at me and with a grin say the usual, "Hello, you devil, you!" I have gotten quite used to it, but at first I wondered how he ever attached that description to a spiritual care coordinator! Then I decided it is probably a term he uses for many others, too! Now, I would be surprised if he didn't greet me this way.

I heard him speak out at a resident council meeting once. His main concern was that he would really be a lot happier if they could just feed him beans and wieners once in a while.

It makes me smile now just to think about it. Surely, on Maslow's *Hierarchy of Needs*, giving one *beans and wieners* to satisfy the basic need for food and shelter would be pretty easy in the scheme of things. If only all our needs could be so easily addressed!

I only saw Pete really melancholy once. He was standing in the lobby, leaning against the window and looking out at the rain. He didn't know I was listening, and, in fact, I felt that if I interrupted him it would be like an invasion of privacy. He was saying, over and over, "Absolutely nothing to do, absolutely nothing to do, absolutely nothing to do."

"…whether we live or die,
we are the Lord's."
—Romans 14:8

Young at Heart

At this time of writing, I am in my mid-fifties. God-willing, I may have another third of life left. Of course, I could die of illness or accident at any moment. I would love to live to see my grandchildren. I would love to see my great-grand-children! But if I were to find out my life was going to be over in twenty-four hours, I think and hope that I am already prepared.

I do long for a new body. I long for a world free of suffering and strife. I long to meet loved ones who have gone on before me. I await the promises of the New Jerusalem! Paul, in his letter to the Romans, said, *"whether we live or die, (we are the winners, because) we are the Lord's!"*

I am not in a hurry to leave this life, as there is still much to experience and enjoy. In many ways, life is good, and I am thankful.

I remember the day when my little brother could beat me up. I remember the day when my son could beat me in a race to the end of the lane. I remember the day when I tried to skip double-dutch and couldn't even enter the ropes. Today, I have the normal aches and pains of a body my age, and can't really run very fast or for very long.

The wonderful thing is this—*inside, I am still young at heart!* In my dreams, I can still run very fast, and do other amazing things! I still have desires and passions for things that are not physically possible anymore! My heart may have aged physically, but spiritually, it has not! One day, when I cross over, I will expect a new, *thin,* healthy body. I will be able to run fast in a race and to skip double-dutch again. As for fighting—I hope I won't have that urge! On that day, my body will match my spirit.

So whether I live or whether I die, I have the victory—*in Christ.* And in this mortal life, as my body ages, I am still *young at heart*. God has given us a human body, but an eternal spirit. Praise be to God!

CASE STUDY

What are the spiritual, physical, intellectual, emotional and social needs of the following person, and how well are they being met?

I am totally bed-bound. I have extensive disease, and am unable to do anything for myself. I have total care provided by the community support worker and the home-care nurse. I am not eating much, and am mostly conscious and coherent, with periods of drowsiness and confusion. I am on several meds for pain and symptom control.

I know I am dying, and have accepted this. I have spoken freely to all members of my family and they are in various stages of acceptance. All are supportive, but handling it differently. My husband is great, and we talk about everything. He is very sad, but compassionate and provides much of my care when the nurses are not here. He will fall apart when I am gone.

I am in a hospital bed in my sunroom. I can see the backyards and fields beyond. I can hear the birds, and the neighbour's dog, and a plane flying overhead. Occasionally I hear a car on the gravel lane, and wonder who has come to see me.

Even though there are pretty flowers on my bedside table, I can smell death all around me—the smell of sickness, stale air and sweat. I smell the soaps and antiseptics, and I imagine I can even smell the medications. Maybe it is my imagination. I wonder if my family can smell it, too, although they don't say anything. I bet even the dog smells death, but he also is too polite to protest, and he lies beside my bed on the mat. He misses our walks.

I try to enjoy bits of food. Sometimes I take in a bit, and sometimes it comes back up. Often, even looking at food is hard. Everyone tries to encourage me to eat. At first I worried about hurting their feelings when they brought my favourite foods, so I would try... but now, I think they get it—I just won't be eating much anymore. A few sips of water or ginger ale seem like a luxury.

I am thinking all kinds of things. I imagine all kinds of scenarios. My mind imagines my death in various ways, and the funeral. I can even imagine my loved ones sad and lonely after I am gone. Why can't my mind be still? I ask God for peace, and sometimes when I am alone I can feel peace, even taste it. Sometimes I feel so ready to let go, and at other times... I am scared.

I don't like a lot of fuss or noise, and ask that my house not turn into chaos. I can't stand chaos—it makes me feel like I'm not in charge. People come and go, and I ask for my favourite music. Not all the time, but a little each day. I have my photo albums beside me, and we take turns looking at them together. At first I did the commentaries myself, but now I am too tired and weak, and someone else must speak the stories. I can only manage ten minutes at a time.

My family asks nothing of me; I hope I have given them what they need. I have given them the blessing, and they have given it back to me. I am fortunate in so many ways. I am ready now to be with the Lord. (Wow, I have heard that cliché before! But it is so true.) I am so tired...

The author can be reached at:
finalscenes@hotmail.ca